DAVID

DAVID
A PLAY

by
D. H. LAWRENCE

**Fredonia Books
Amsterdam, The Netherlands**

David

by
D. H. Lawrence

ISBN: 1-58963-711-9

Copyright © 2002 by Fredonia Books

Reprinted from the 1926 edition

Fredonia Books
Amsterdam, The Netherlands
http://www.fredoniabooks.com

All rights reserved, including the right to reproduce this book, or portions thereof, in any form.

In order to make original editions of historical works available to scholars at an economical price, this facsimile of the original edition of 1926 is reproduced from the best available copy and has been digitally enhanced to improve legibility, but the text remains unaltered to retain historical authenticity.

CHARACTERS

DAVID, *son of Jesse.*
SAUL, *King of Israel.*
SAMUEL, *Prophet of God.*
JONATHAN, *son of Saul.*
ABNER, *leader of Saul's host.*
AGAG, *King of Amalek.*
MERAB, *daughter of Saul.*
MICHAL, *daughter of Saul.*
WOMAN-SERVANT.
MAIDENS.
JESSE, *father of David.*
ELIAB, ABINADAB, SHAMMAH, *brothers of David.*
FOURTH, FIFTH, SIXTH, AND SEVENTH BROTHERS *of David.*
ADRIEL THE MEHOLATHITE.
Captains, fighting-men, herald, armour-bearer, elders, neighbours, Prophets, herdsmen, and lad.

DAVID

SCENE I

Courtyard of SAUL's *house in Gilgal: sort of compound with an adobe house beyond.* AGAG, *bound, seated on the ground, and fastened by a rope to a post of the shed. Men with spears. Enter* MERAB *and* MICHAL, *daughters of* SAUL, *with tambourines.* MAIDENS.

MERAB [*running and dancing*]: Saul came home with the spoil of the Amalekite.
MAIDENS: Hie! Amalekite! Hie! Amalekite!
MICHAL: Saul threw his spear into the desert of Shur, through the heart of the Amalekite.
MAIDENS: Stuck the Amalekite, pierced him to the ground.
MICHAL: Wind of the desert blows between the ribs of Amalek, only the jackal is fat on that land. Who smote the Amalekite, as a sand-storm smites the desert?
MAIDENS: Saul! Saul! Saul is the slayer and the death of Amalek.
MERAB [*before* AGAG]: What is this dog with a string round his neck?
MAIDENS: What dog is this?
MICHAL: I know this dog, men used to call it King!
MAIDENS: Look at this King!
MERAB: Agag, Agag, King of the Amalekites! Dog on a string at the heel of mighty Saul!

MICHAL [*speaking to* AGAG]: Are you the King of the Amalekites?

AGAG: I am he, maiden!

MICHAL: I thought it was a dog my father had brought home, and tied to a post.

MERAB: Why are you alone, Agag? Where are all your armed men, that ran like lions round the road to Egypt? Where are your women, with gold on their foreheads? Let us hear the tinkle of the bracelets of your women, O King, King Agag, King of mighty Amalek!

MAIDENS: [*laughing—shaking tambourines in* AGAG's *face—spitting on him*]: Dog! Dog! Dog of an Amalekite!

MICHAL: Who hung on the heels of Israel when they journeyed out of the wilderness of Shur, coming from Egypt, in the days of our fathers, in the day of Moses our great deliverer?

MAIDENS: Ay! Ay! Who threw their spears in the backs of the wandering Israelites?

MICHAL: Who killed our women, and the weary ones, and the heavy-footed, in the bitter days of wandering, when we came up out of Egypt?

MERAB: Who among our enemies was accursed like the Amalekite? When Moses held the rod of God uplifted in his hand, Joshua smote the Amalekite till the sun went down. But even when the sun was gone, came the voice of the Almighty: *War, and war with Amalek, till Amalek is put out from under heaven.*

MICHAL: Dog! Son of dogs that lay in wait for us as we passed by! Dog! Why has Saul left you eyes to see, and ears to hear!

Scene I   DAVID   5

SAUL [*coming from house*]: AGAG is among the maidens!

MICHAL: See, Father, is *this* a king?

SAUL: Even so.

MICHAL: It is a dog that cannot scratch his own fleas.

SAUL: Even so, it is a king: King of rich Amalek. Have you seen the presents he has brought for the household of Saul?

MICHAL: For the daughters of Saul, Father?

SAUL: Surely for Merab and Michal, daughters of Saul. [*To a man.*] Ho! Bring the basket of spoils for the daughters of the King.

MICHAL: Listen! Listen! King Agag seeks a wife in Gilgal! Oh, Father, I do not like him! He looks like a crow the dogs have played with. Merab, here is a King for your hand!

MERAB: Death is his portion, the Amalekite.

MICHAL: Will you put him to death, Father? Let us laugh a little longer at his Amalek nose.

[*Enter man with basket—also* JONATHAN *and* ABNER.]

SAUL: See the gifts of Agag, King of Amalek, to the daughters of Saul! Tissue from Egypt, head-veils from Pharaoh's house! And see, red robes from Tyre, and yellow from Sidon.

MICHAL [*screams*]: That for *me*, Father, that for me! Give the other to Merab.—Ah! Ah! Ah!—Thank you, King Agag; thank you, King of Amalek.

SAUL: Goldsmith's work for arms and ankles, gold and dropping silver, for the ears.

MICHAL: Give me those! Give me those! Give the others to Merab! Ay! Ay! Maidens! How am I?— See, Agag, noble Agag, how am I now? Listen!

[*She dances, the ornaments clink.*] They say: *Noble Agag!—King of Givers!* Poor draggled crow that had gold in its nest! Caw! King Agag! Caw! It's a daughter of Saul, of long-limbed Saul, smiter of Amalek, who tinkles with joys of the Amalekite.

JONATHAN: Peace, maiden! Go in and spin wool with the women. You are too much among the men.

MICHAL: Art thou speaking, O Jonathan, full of thy own manhood?

JONATHAN: Take in these spoils from the eye of men, and the light of day. Father, there came one saying that Samuel sought you in Carmel.

SAUL: Let him find me in Gilgal.

ABNER: They are calling even now at the gate.

[*Moves to gate.*]

SAUL [*to girls*]: Go to the house and hide your spoil, for if this prophet of prophets finds the treasure of the Amalekite upon you, he will tear it away, and curse your youth.

MICHAL: That he shall not! Oh, Merab, you got the blue shawl from me! Run! Maidens! Run! Farewell, King Agag, your servant thanks your lordship! —Caw!—Nay, he cannot even say caw!

[*Exit—running—*MICHAL, *and other* MAIDENS *follow.*]

ABNER: It is so, my lord. Samuel even now has passed the stone of directions, seeking Saul in Gilgal.

SAUL: It is well. He has come to bless our triumph.

JONATHAN: Father, will you leave that man in the sight of Samuel?

SAUL: No! Go you quickly into the house, O Agag! Take him quickly, men, and let no mouth speak his name.

[*Exeunt* AGAG *and men.*]

JONATHAN: I have a misgiving, Father, that Samuel comes not in peace, after Saul in Gilgal.
SAUL: Has Saul laid low the Amalekite, to fear the coming of an old prophet?
ABNER: Samuel is a jealous man, full of the tyranny of prophecy. Shall we wait him here, or go into the house and be seated on the mats? Or shall we go forth from the gate towards him?
SAUL: I will stay here, and brighten my sword-edge in the waiting.
ABNER [*at the gate—calling*]: He is coming across the field; an old man in a mantle, alone, followed by two of his prophets.
JONATHAN [*joining* ABNER]: It is he. And coming in anger.
ABNER: In anger against whom?
JONATHAN: Against my father. Because we have not destroyed the Amalekite utterly, but have saved the best spoil.
ABNER: Nay, but it is a foolish thing, to throw fine linen into the fire, and fat young oxen down a dry well.
JONATHAN: It was the commandment.
ABNER: Why should the maidens not rejoice in their ornaments, and the God of the Unknown Name enjoy the scent of blood-sacrifice?

[*They retreat from the gate;* SAUL *sharpens his sword. After a pause, enter* SAMUEL, *followed by the prophets.*]

SAUL [*laying down his sword*]: Blessed be thou of the Lord! I have performed the commandment of the Lord.
SAMUEL: What meaneth the bleating of the sheep in

my ears, and the lowing of the oxen which I hear?
SAUL: They have brought them from the Amalekites. The people spared the best of the sheep, and of the oxen, to sacrifice unto thy God, but the rest we have utterly destroyed.
SAMUEL: Stay, and I will tell thee what I have heard out of the inner darkness, this night.
SAUL: Say on.
SAMUEL: When thou wast little in thine own sight, wast thou not made the chieftain of the tribes of Israel, and the Deep poured his power over thee, to anoint thee King? And the Voice out of the deeps sent thee on a journey, saying: Go, and utterly destroy the sinners the Amalekites, and fight against them until they be consumed.—Why then did you not obey the Voice, instead of flying upon the spoil, and doing evil in the sight of the Unclosing Eyes?
SAUL: Yea, I have obeyed the Voice from the beyond. I have gone the way which the Great One sent me, and have brought Agag the King of Amalek prisoner, and have utterly destroyed the Amalekites. But the people took the spoil, sheep and oxen, the chief of the things which should have been utterly destroyed, to sacrifice in Gilgal unto the Lord thy God.
SAMUEL: Does the Breather of the skies take as great delight in sacrifice and burnt offerings as in obedience to the Voice that spoke on the breath of the night? Behold, to obey is better than sacrifice, and to hearken than the fat of rams.
SAUL: Is not God the sender of life, and the bread of life? And shall we deny the meat and destroy the bread that is sent?

SAMUEL: Behold, is the Lord my God a sutler, to stock the larders of Saul? Lo, He heeds not the fat beef nor the fine raiment, but threshes out His anger in the firmament. Amalek has defied the living Breath, and cried mockery on the Voice of the Beyond. Therefore the living Wrath will wipe out the Amalekite, by the hand of His servant, Israel. And if the Nameless is without compunction, whence the compunction of Saul?

SAUL: I feared the people, and obeyed their voice.

SAMUEL: Yea, that was bravely done! Thou didst not fear the Great Lord, thou fearest the people, smaller than thyself. Thou didst not obey the Cry from the midst of the dark, but the voice of the people!—I tell thee, rebellion is as the sin of witchcraft, and stubbornness is as iniquity and idolatry. Because thou hast rejected the word of the Lord, the Lord hath also rejected thee from being King.

SAUL: Shall a King not hearken to the voice of his people?

SAMUEL: The people cried for a King, in the frowardness of their hearts. But can they make a King out of one of themselves? Can they whistle a lion forth from a litter of dogs? The people cried for a King, and the Lord gave to them. Even thee, Saul. But why art thou King! Because of the voice of the people?

SAUL: Thou didst choose me out.

SAMUEL: The finger of the Thunder pointed me to thee, and the Wind of Strength blew me in thy way. And thou art King because from out of the middle world the great Wish settled upon thee. And thou art King because the Lord poured the oil of His might over thee. But thou art disobedient, and shut-test thine ears to the Voice. Thou hearest the barkings of dogs and the crying of the people, and the Voice of the Midmost is nothing to thee. Therefore thou hast become as nothing unto the Lord, and He that chose thee rejecteth thee again. The power of the Lord shall fall away from thee, and thou shalt become again a common man, and a little thing, as when the Lord first found thee.

SAUL: I have sinned. For I have transgressed the commandments of the Lord, which thou didst hear out of the deeps of the night. Because I feared the people, and obeyed their voice. But now, I pray thee, pardon my sin, and turn again with me, that I may find the Lord, to worship Him.

SAMUEL: I will not return with thee: for thou hast rejected the word of the Lord, and the Lord hath rejected thee from being King over Israel. [SAMUEL *turns away.* SAUL *catches hold of the hem of* SAMUEL'S *garment and it tears in his hand.*] The Lord hath rent the Kingdom of Israel away from thee this day, and hath given it to a neighbour of thine, that is better than thou [*pause*];—and the Mighty One that moveth Israel will not lie, nor repent towards thee again: for He is not a man that He should repent.

SAUL. I have sinned, I have sinned, I have turned my face the wrong way. Yet honour me now, I pray thee! Honour me before the elders of my people, and before Israel, and turn again with me, that I may find the Lord thy God, and worship Him.

SAMUEL [*turning*]: Thou hast turned away from the Hidden Sun, and the gleam is dying from out of thy face. Thou hast disowned the Power that made thee, and the glow is leaving thy limbs, the glisten of oil is waning on thy brow, and the vision is dying in thy breast. Yet because thou art the Lord's anointed I will bless thee again in the sight of the elders. Yet if the Lord hath decided against thee, what avails an old man's blessing?

SAUL: Yet bless me, my Father.

SAMUEL [*lifting his hand*]: The Lord be with thee! The Lord's strength strengthen thee! The power and the might of the Lord brighten thine eyes and light thy face: the Lord's life lift thy limbs and gladden the walls of thy breast, and put power in thy belly and thy hips! The Lord's haste strengthen thy knees and quicken thy feet!

SAUL [*lifting both hands to heaven*]: Lo, I have sinned, and lost myself, I have been mine own undoing. But I turn again to Innermost, where the flame is, and the wings are throbbing. Hear me, take me back! Brush me again with the wings of life, breathe on me with the breath of Thy desire, come in unto me, and be with me, and dwell in me. For without the presence of the awful Lord, I am an empty shell. Turn to me, and fill my heart, and forgive my transgression. For I will wash myself clean of Amalek, to the last speck, and remove the source of my sinning [*drops his hands—turns to* SAMUEL.] Is it well, O Samuel!

SAMUEL: May it be well! Bring me hither Agag, King of the Amalekites.

SAUL: Ho, Jonathan, send here Agag the Amalekite. And send thou the chief of the herdsmen, O Abner, for we must wipe away the stain of Amalek swiftly, out of Gilgal.

[*Exeunt* JONATHAN *and* ABNER.]

SAUL: [*to* SAMUEL]: The Lord shall be with me again this day, that the Kingdom be not rent from me.

SAMUEL: Who knoweth the ways of the Deep? I will entreat, ah! for thee in the night-time, and in the day. But if He hath turned His face away, what am I but an old man crying like an infant in the night!

[*Enter* AGAG—*coming forward delicately.*]

AGAG: Surely the bitterness of death is past.

SAMUEL [*seizing* SAUL's *sword*]: As thy sword hath made women childless, so shall thy mother be childless among women. [*Rushes on* AGAG *with sword*— AGAG *steps behind a wall*, SAMUEL *upon him.*]

[*Enter* HERDSMAN.]

JONATHAN: Better it had been in battle, on the field of the fight.

ABNER: It is a sacrifice.

SAUL [*to* HERDSMAN]: Gather together the cattle of the Amalekite which came as spoil, and fasten them in a pen. Leave out no sheep and no calf, nor any goat, but put them all in.

HERDSMAN: It shall be as Saul says.

[*Exit.*]

SAMUEL [*entering with red sword*]: I have hewed him in pieces before the Lord, and his blood has gone up to the Most High; it is in the nostrils of the God of Wrath.

SAUL: Come now, I pray thee, within the house, and let them bring water for thy feet and food to gladden thine heart.

SAMUEL: It may not be. But I must go to Ramah to entreat for thee before the Lord, and even now must I go. And may the Might be with thee.

CURTAIN

SCENE II

A room in Ramah. Night. SAMUEL *in prayer.*

SAMUEL: Speak to me out of the whirlwind, come to me from behind the sun, listen to me where the winds are hastening. When the power of the whirlwind moves away from me, I am a worthless old man. Out of the deep of deeps comes a breath upon me, and my old flesh freshens like a flower. I know no age. Oh, upon the wings of distance turn to me, send the fanning strength into my hips. I am sore for Saul, and my old bones are weary for the King. My heart is like a fledgling in a nest, abandoned by its mother. My heart opens its mouth with vain cries, weak and meaningless, and the Mover of the deeps will not stoop to me. My bowels are twisted in a knot of grief, in a knot of anguish for my son, for him whom I anointed beneath the firmament of might. On earth move men and beasts, they nourish themselves and know not how they are alive. But in all the places moves Unseen Almighty, like a breath among the stars, or the moon, like the sea turning herself over. I eat bread, but my soul faints, and wine will not heal my bones. Nothing is good for me but God. Like waters He moves through the world, like a fish I swim in the flood of God Himself. Answer me, Mover of the waters, speak to me as waves speak without mouths. Saul has fallen off, as a ripe fig falls and bursts. He, anointed, he moved in the flood of power, he was God's, he was not his own. Now he is cast up like a fish among the dry stones, he beats himself against the sun-licked pebbles. He jumped out from the deeps of the Lord, the sea of God has seen him depart. He will die within the smell of his own violence. Lord, Lord, Ocean and Mover of oceans, lick him into the flood of Thyself. Wilt Thou not reach for him with the arm of a long wave, and catch him back into the deeps of living God? Is he lost from the sway of the tide for ever and for ever? When the rain wets him, will it wet him Godless, and will the wind blow on him without God in it? Lord, wilt Thou not reach for him, he is Thine anointed? Bitter are the waters of old age, and tears fall inward on the heart. Saul is the son whom I anointed, and Saul has crawled away from God, he creeps up the rocks in vanity, the stink of him will rise up like a dead crab. Lord, is it verily so with Saul, is he gone out from Thee for ever, like a creeping thing crawled in vanity from the element of elements? I am old, and my tears run inward, they deaden my heart because of Saul. For Saul has crawled away from the Fountain of Days, and the Ancient of Days will know him no more. I hear the voice of the Lord like waters washing through the night, saying: *Saul has fallen away and is no more in the way of the power of God.* Yea, what is love, that I should love him! He is fallen away, and stinketh like a dead crab, and my love stinks with him. I must wash myself because of Saul, and strip myself of him again, and go down into the deeps of God. Speak, Lord, and I will obey. Tell me, and I will do it. I sink like a stone in the sea, and nothing of my own is left me. I am gone away from myself, I disappear in the deeps of God. And the oracle of the Lord stirs me, as the fountains of the deep. Lo! I am not mine own. The flood has covered me and the waters of the beginning sound in the shell of my heart. And I will find another King for Israel, I shall know him by the whispers of my heart. Lo, I will fill the horn with oil again, with the oil from the body of Him, and I will go into the hills of Judah. I will find out one, in whom the power sleeps. And I will pour potency over his head and anoint him with God's fecundity, and place him beyond forgetting. I will go into the hills of Judah, where the sheep feed among the rocks, and find a man fresh in the morning of God. And he shall be King. On the morrow I will gather myself and go, silently, carrying the kingship away from Saul, because the virtue is gone out of him. And Saul will kill me with a spear, in one stroke, for rage he will kill me, if I tell him. But I shall not tell him. I shall say: I must away to the land of Judah, it is the time to sacrifice in the place of Bethlehem, the appointed time is at hand.—So I shall go away from Saul for ever, and never shall I see his face again. I shall hide myself away from his face, lest he hurt himself, slaying me. I shall go in the morning with sure feet, but the shell of my heart will be weary. For I am the Lord's and servant of the Lord, and I go in obedience, even with the alacrity of willingness. But alas, that I should have loved Saul, and had pride in him! I am old.

CURTAIN

SCENE III

Bethlehem: an open place in the village. An old man on a roof calling aloud and kindling a signal fire.

1ST ELDER [*calling, on the roof*]: Come in! Come in! Come in! Come all men in! Come all in to the place of counsel! Gather into the place of counsel, all men gather now. Come in! Come in!
2ND ELDER [*on the plaza*]: What now?
3RD ELDER: The watchman on the fourth hill saw a host of prophets coming, even Samuel among them.
2ND ELDER: Yea! What does this bode?
JESSE: What have we done wrong, that Samuel comes down upon us? If he curses us we are dead men.
4TH ELDER: Dread is on me. The sun looks darkened.
3RD ELDER: Nay, let us wait. It may be he comes in peace.
ELIAB [*brother of* DAVID]: Who do we, who are men that fear not the lion nor the bear, nor even the Philistine, tremble before the raging of these prophets?
2ND ELDER: Hush then! For the Bolt is above us, and can strike out of a clear sky. Canst thou hear His meaning, or know His vision, Who is secret save to the prophets? Peace then, hush thy mouth.
JESSE: Verily, there is no open vision, and the word of One is precious. Without Samuel, we should stare with the stare of deaf men, and the fixed eyes of the

blind. We should run our faces against the wall, and fall with our feet into a hole. We should not hear the lion roaring upon us.

ELIAB: Not so, my Father. Without a prophet I seek the lion when he roars about the herd, I slay him without advice from the Lord. We live our lives as men, by the strength of our right hand. Why heed the howlings of priests in linen ephods, one or many!

JESSE: My son, shut thy teeth on such words. Seal thy heart to silence. The strength of a man lasts for a little time, and wastes like the oil in a lamp. You are young, and your lamp is unbroken. But those that live long needs must renew their strength again, and have their vessel replenished. And only from the middle-middle of all the worlds, where God stirs amid His waters, can strength come to us.

ELIAB: Will it not come without Samuel?

JESSE: There is a path that the gazelle cannot follow, and the lion knows not, nor can the eagle fly it. Rare is the soul of the prophet, that can find the hidden path of the Lord. There is no open vision, and we, who can see the lion in the thicket, cannot see the Lord in the darkness, nor hear Him out of the cloud. But the word of One is precious, and we perish without it.

ELIAB: *I* cannot bow my heart to Samuel. Is he a King to lead us into battle, and share the spoil with us? Why should we fare worse without him?

JESSE: My son, day follows day, and night travels between the days. But the heart of man cannot wander among the years like a wild ass in the wilderness, running hither and thither. The heart at last stands still, crying: *Whither? Whither?* Like a lost foal whinnying for his dam, the heart cries and nickers for God, and will not be comforted. Then comes the prophet with the other vision in his eyes, and the inner hearing in his ears, and he uncovers the secret path of the Lord, Who is at the middlemost place of all. And when the heart is in the way of God, it runs softly and joyously, without weariness.

ELIAB: I would sooner follow the King, with spear and shield.

JESSE: Samuel is more precious than the King, and more to be obeyed. As God is to Samuel, Samuel to the King is God. The King is as a boy awaiting his father's bidding, uneasy till he is told what he shall do. Even so Samuel speaks to Saul, with the mouth of authority, to be obeyed. For he is the lips of God.

ELIAB: For me, give me the right arm of Saul.

[SAMUEL *enters—followed by wild prophets. The* ELDERS *go to meet him.*]

1ST ELDER: The Lord be with thee!

SAMUEL: The Lord keep this people!

1ST ELDER: Comest thou in peace?

SAMUEL: In peace. I come to sacrifice unto the Lord. Sanctify yourselves and come to sacrifice, according to your families. Renew your clothes and purify yourselves.

1ST ELDER: Into which house will you go?

SAMUEL: Into the house of Jesse.

JESSE: I am here, my lord.

SAMUEL: Call your household together, and sanctify yourselves, for we will sacrifice a heifer to the Lord this day, in your house. And it shall be a feast unto you.

CURTAIN

SCENE IV

JESSE's *house. A small inner courtyard: a rude altar smoking, and blood sprinkled round:* **SAMUEL** *before the altar, hands bloody. In another part a large red fire with a great pot seething, and pieces of meat roasting on spits.* **JESSE** *turning the spits. It is evening, sun going down.*

SAMUEL: Call your sons. Call them one by one to pass before me. For I will look on them, before we sit around to the feast of the sacrifice.

JESSE: They are in the house, waiting. I will call the first-born first. [*Calling.*] Eliab, come forth! Samuel asks for thee!

ELIAB [*entering*]: The Lord be with you.

SAMUEL [*aside*]: Surely the Lord's anointed is before Him! [*Gazes at* ELIAB *who is big and handsome.*]

SAMUEL [*aside*]: I shall not look on his countenance, nor on the height of his stature. For the voice of my soul tells me he is rejected. The Lord sees not as men see. For man looketh on the outward appearance, but the Lord looketh on the heart.

SAMUEL [*to* JESSE]: Him hath the Lord not chosen. Call thy other son.

JESSE: Ha! Abinadab! And Eliab, gather all thy brothers together, for the feast shall be set forth.

[*Exit* ELIAB.]

ABINADAB [*entering*]: The Lord be with you.

SAMUEL [*gazing on* ABINADAB]: Neither hath the Lord chosen this.
JESSE: Go thou, Abinadab! Be all thy brethren ready in the house?
ABINADAB: They be all there, waiting for the sacrifice meat.
JESSE [*calling*]: Come, Shammah! And when I call, come you others in your order, one by one.
SHAMMAH [*entering*]: The Lord be with you.
SAMUEL [*slowly*]: Neither hath the Lord chosen this.
JESSE: Go thou! Nay! Rather go to the fire and turn the spitted meat.
SHAMMAH: Yea! For it should not singe.
JESSE [*calling*]: Ho! Son! Come forward!
FOURTH SON: The Lord be with you!
SAMUEL: Neither hath the Lord chosen this.
JESSE: Go thou hence, and wait yet a while.
FOURTH SON: What wouldst thou then with me?
JESSE [*calling*]: Ho! Son! [*To him who waits.*] Nay, go or stay, as thou wilt. But stand aside. [*He stands aside.*]
FIFTH SON: The Lord be with you.
JESSE: Turn thy face to the sun, that it may be seen.
SAMUEL: Neither hath the Lord chosen this.
JESSE: Thou art not he, whom Samuel seeks. Stand thou aside. [*Calling.*] Ho! Son! [*To him who waits.*] Bring in thy brother.

[*Enter* SIXTH SON: *all the other brothers edge in after him.*]

SIXTH SON: The Lord be with you!
SAMUEL: Neither hath the Lord chosen this.
SIXTH SON: Wherefore hast thou called me, my Father?
JESSE: Samuel would look on the faces of all my sons.

Go now! Who then was not called? Who among you has not come forward?

SEVENTH SON: I! Wilt thou me?

JESSE: Nay, but come into the light before the prophet of God.

SAMUEL: Neither hath the Lord chosen this.

JESSE: Nay, then it is finished, for there be no more.

SAMUEL: Are here all thy children?

JESSE: Yea, verily, there remaineth yet the youngest. And behold, he keepeth the sheep.

SAMUEL: Send and fetch him. For we will not sit down till he come hither.

JESSE: Go thou, Shammah, for he will be coming in now. I will see——!

[*Exit* JESSE, *also* SHAMMAH.]

ELIAB: My lord, will the Lord of Hosts anoint a King, while Saul yet liveth?

SAMUEL: My son, out of the deep cloud the lightning cometh, and toucheth its own. Even so, from the whirlwind of the whole world's middle, leaneth out the Wonderful and toucheth His own, but whether the anointing be for prophecy or priesthood, or for a leader or a King over Israel, the Mover of all hath it in His own deeps.

ELIAB: Yea! But if the Lord anoint a man to be King, can the Lord again take back the anointing, and wipe out the oil, and remove the gift, and undo the man He has made?

SAMUEL: The power is beyond us, both before and after. Am I not anointed before the people? But if I should say: *The power is my own; I will even do my own bidding*, then this is the sin of witchcraft, which stealeth the power of the whirlwind for its own. And the power will be taken from me, and I shall fall into a pit.

ELIAB: It is a hard thing, to be the Lord's anointed.

SAMUEL: For the froward and irreverent spirit, it is a thing well-nigh impossible.

[*Enter* JESSE *with* DAVID.]

JESSE: This is David, the last of the sons of Jesse.

[*Enter* SHAMMAH.]

SAMUEL [*aside*]: I shall arise and anoint him. For this is he. [*Aloud.*] The Lord hath chosen this one. [*Takes the horn of oil and holds it over* DAVID's *head.*] The skies will anoint thee with their glory, the oil of the Sun is poured over thee, and the strength of His power. Thou shalt be a master of the happenings among men. Answer then. Does thy soul go forth to the Deep, does the Wonderer move in thy soul?

DAVID: Yea, my lord. Surely my soul leaps with God!

SAMUEL [*anointing* DAVID]: The Glory pours Himself out on thee. The Chooser chooseth thee. Thou shalt be no more thine own, for the chosen belongs to the Chooser. When thou goeth in, it shall be at the whisper of the Mover, and when thou comest out, it shall be the Lord. Thy strength is at the heart of the world, and thy desires are from thence. The walls of thy breast are the front of the Lord, thy loins are the Deep's, and the fire within them is His. The Lord looketh out of thy eyes and sits on thy lips. Thou closest thy fist on the Deep, and thy knees smile with His strength. He holdeth the bow of thy body erect, and thy thighs are the pillars of His presence. Henceforward thou are not thine own. The Lord is upon thee, and thou art His.

DAVID [*making an obeisance*]: I am thy servant, my lord.

SAMUEL: Ye shall sit around, and divide the meat, and eat of the feast, and bid the neighbours to your feast of sacrifice this night.

   [*They move around, fetching trenchers of wood, and a huge dish, and a heap of flat bread. They begin to take the meat from the fire, and with a cry lift down the pot.*]

JESSE: David is a child, and the Lord hath chosen him. What shall become of him? Make it plain to us, O Samuel, this night!

SAMUEL: Ask not, for none knoweth. Let him live till such time as the Unseen stretcheth out His hands upon him. When the time is fulfilled, then we shall know. Beforehand no man knoweth. And now the meat is ready from the fire, and the feast of sacrifice is prepared, and I have done. Eat you of the feast, and live before the Lord, and be blessed. Speak nothing of this hour, lest mischance befall you. I go my way. Do not seek to stay me. Call whom ye will to meat, eat then what is before you, for this is your hour.

JESSE: The sun has gone down, and it is night. Wilt thou verily go forth?

   [*Exit* SAMUEL.]

ELIAB: He has anointed the youngest, and the oldest he has passed over.

JESSE: It is the Lord. Go, Abinadab, and bid in the neighbours to the feast.

ELIAB: Nay, it is Samuel, who envies a strong man his strength, and settles on the weak.

JESSE: These things, at this hour, thou shalt not say. Is

my son David chosen beneath the heavens, and shall Eliab his brother cast it up a reproach to him? Yea! pile up the dish from the pot, that it may cool, and not burn the hand of him that tasteth.

ELIAB [*to* DAVID]: Wilt thou be a priest in a blue ephod?

DAVID: I know not. To-day and to-morrow I shall keep my father's sheep. More I know not.

ELIAB: Canst thou see the Bolt within the cloud? Canst thou hear His voice out of the ground?

DAVID: I know not. I wish the Lord be with me.

ELIAB: Is He nearer thee, than thine own father?

DAVID: My father sits before me and I see his face. But the Lord is in my limbs as a wind in a tree, and the tree is shaken.

ELIAB: Is not the Lord also in me, thou stripling? Is thine the only body that is visited?

DAVID: I know not. My own heart I know. Thou knowest thine own. I wish the Lord be with me.

ELIAB: Yea, I know my own heart indeed. Neither is it the heart of a whelp that minds the sheep, but the heart of a man that holds a spear. Canst thou draw my bow, or wield my sword?

DAVID: My day is not yet come.

JESSE: It is enough. The guests we have bidden are here! O David, my son, even carry out their portion to the womenfolk, for they may not come here. And think thou no more of this day. The Lord will move in His own time, thou canst not hasten Him. [*To the* NEIGHBOURS.] Nay, come! And sit ye to meat! For we will eat this night of the sacrifice that Samuel hath slain before the Lord.

NEIGHBOURS: Peace be to this house! And is Samuel at

once gone forth? Yea! Good seemeth thy feast, O Jesse!

JESSE: An heifer, of the first year, fat and goodly! Reach forth thy hand.

    [*They all sit around the huge, smoking platter.* JESSE *dips in his hand, and carries the mess to his mouth.*]

NEIGHBOUR: Yea! Good is the feast! And blessed be Samuel, who came to Bethlehem this day! [*Re-enter* DAVID: *sits down and eats. They all dip their hands in the great platter, and eat in silence.*] Verily, this is a great feast! Surely the Lord hath visited thy house this day, O Jesse!

CURTAIN

SCENE V

SAUL'S *house in Gilgal.* MERAB *and* MICHAL *in the courtyard, spinning wool, with their maidens. They are laughing and giggling.*

1ST MAIDEN: Now I'll ask one! I'll ask one.
MERAB: Ask then!
3RD MAIDEN: Why does a cow look over a wall?
MICHAL: Yah! Yah! We know that old one. We all know it.
MERAB: Who knows the answer? Hold your hand up.
   [*Only* MICHAL *holds up her hand.*]
3RD MAIDEN: There! There! They don't know it! Why does a cow look over a wall?
1ST MAIDEN: To see what's on the other side.
MICHAL: Wrong! Wrong! How silly! [*Laughter.*]
2ND MAIDEN: Because it wants to get out.
MICHAL: Wrong! And it's such an easy one.
3RD MAIDEN: Why does a cow look over a wall?
4TH MAIDEN: To scratch its neck.   [*Much laughter.*]
3RD MAIDEN: Wrong! Wrong! All wrong! Give it up!
MICHAL: No! No! Let them guess again. Why does a cow look over a wall?
1ST MAIDEN: To see if David's coming to drive her to pasture. [*Wild laughter.*]
MICHAL: That's wrong! That's not the answer!
MERAB: Give it up?

3RD MAIDEN [*laughing wildly*]: *To see if David's coming to drive her to pasture!*

MICHAL: That's not the answer, *Stupid!*

1ST MAIDEN: Why not, say I? It's as good as the real answer.—The cows of Jesse will have to look a long time over a wall. [*Much laughter.*] No doubt they're looking at this moment. [*Shrieks of laughter.*] Mooo-oo! Moo-oo! David, come home. [*Hysterical laughter.*]

MICHAL: Fool! Fool! That's not the answer.

1ST MAIDEN: Yes. That's the answer in Bethlehem. Why does a Bethlehem cow look over a wall?—Because David's come to Gilgal. [*Much laughter.*]

MICHAL: That's wrong! That's wrong!

2ND MAIDEN: It's not wrong for a Bethlehem cow.

MICHAL: But it's not a Bethlehem cow. [*Much laughter.*]

1ST MAIDEN: Is it the heifers of Gilgal? [*Wild laughter.*]

4TH MAIDEN: Why do the heifers of King Saul look over the wall in Gilgal?

1ST MAIDEN: Listening to the music. [*Wild laughter.*]

MERAB [*amid her laughter*]: If my father hears us!

MICHAL: You are all fools! You don't know the right answer. You can't guess it! You can't guess it.

2ND MAIDEN: Well, what is it then? Only Michal knows what the cow is looking for! [*Laughter.*]

MAIDENS: Go on! Go on! Tell us, Michal!

MICHAL: Because she can't see through it. [*Laughter.*]

1ST MAIDEN: See through what? [*Wild laughter.*]

MAIDENS: See through what? [*All laughing.*]

2ND MAIDEN: Because who can't see through what? [*Shrieks of laughter.*]

1ST MAIDEN: What a senseless answer! *Because she can't see through it!* [*Shrieks of laughter.*]

MICHAL: You are all fools! fools! fools! You know *nothing*. You don't know *anything*.

[*Enter* SAUL—*angry.*]

SAUL: Enough! Enough! What is all this? Is there a madness among the women? Silence, I say!

MICHAL: We are but telling riddles.

SAUL: It shall not be! What! am I to hear the shrieks of my daughters' folly spoiling the morning? I will riddle you a riddle you shall not care for. [MAIDENS *steal away.*]

MERAB: We had thought my father was abroad among the men.

SAUL: You had thought, had you! And your father's being abroad was timely to let loose your ribaldry!

MICHAL: Nay, Father, there was no ribaldry. The maid did only ask, Why does a cow look over a wall?

SAUL [*shouting*]: Be still! Or I will run this spear through your body. Am I to wrestle with the Lord and fail because of the wantoning of my daughters among their maidens! Oh! cursed in my offspring as in all things! [MERAB *steals away.*] Cursed above all my womenfolk!

MICHAL: Could we not help you, Father, to strive with the Lord? They say the wise women can command the spirits of the deep.

SAUL: Art thou then a seeress? art thou amongst the witches?

MICHAL: Not so. But Saul my father is among the wondrous. Should not his daughter be as wise as the wise women who can see into the mysteries?

SAUL [*groaning*]: This is the sin of witchcraft! The hand of my children is against me!

MICHAL: Nay, Father, we would indeed be for you, and not against you.

SAUL: I have sworn to wipe out the sin of witchcraft from the land, I have sworn the death of all who lure the people with spirits and with wizardry. I have killed the soothsayers in the towns and the villages.

MICHAL: But, Father, might I not see the Bolt in a cloud, or call the Spirits out of the earth! I am your daughter—is that to be a witch?

SAUL: Thou art a spawn of evil, and I will run thee through.

MICHAL: But why! Oh why!

SAUL: Thy soul is a soul of a witch that workest against thy father. I call on the Lord, and my heart foams, because He will not hear me. I know it now. It is thee, thou witch! [*Wanting to strike her with the spear.*]

MICHAL [*weeping*]: It is not so! It is not so! The people say of thee, the Lord has departed from thee, and I would only help thee with the Lord, as Jonathan helps thee against the Philistines.

SAUL [*horrified*]: Is the Deep a Philistine! Nay, now I know thou art the brood of witches, who catch the powers of the earth by cunning. Now I will surely pierce thee through, that my house may be pure, and the Fire may look on me again.

MICHAL [*screams*]: My lord! My lord!

SAUL: I will pierce thee through. For I have sworn the death of all witches, and such as steal the powers of earth and sky by their cunning. It will be as good a deed in the sight of the Lord, as when the prophet of God slew Agag, and Samuel will turn to me again. For I am empty when the Lord abandons me. And evil spirits break into my empty place, and torture me.—I will surely slay this witch, though she were seven times my youngest. For she lifts the latch to the evil spirit that gets into my soul unawares.

MICHAL: My lord! My lord! I am no witch! I am not!

SAUL: Thou art a witch, and thy hand worketh against me, even when thou knowest not. Nay, thou art a witch and thy soul worketh witchcraft even when thou sleepest. Therefore I will pierce thee through. And I will say unto the people: Saul hath slain the witch that gnawed nearest into his heart.

MICHAL: I will not be slain! [*Shrieks.*]

[*Enter* JONATHAN *and* DAVID, *running.*]

JONATHAN: My Father!

DAVID: O King!

SAUL: This is the witch that hinders me with the Lord!

JONATHAN: This, Father! Why, Michal is a child, what can she know of witchcraft?

SAUL: It is in her will. My soul tells me that women with their evil intentions are playing against me, with the Lord. And this is she. She shall die as the others, seeresses, died, to cleanse the land before the Lord God.

DAVID: But yet, O King, thy servant has heard it is a hard thing to be a witch, a work of silent labour and of years. And this maiden your daughter is not silent, I think, nor does she seem to waste her young brows in secret labours.

JONATHAN: That is true enough. She is a feather-brain.

SAUL: Yet is her spirit against her father's.

MICHAL [*still weeping*]: No! No! I would help him.
DAVID: If some spirit of evil hinder King Saul with the Lord of Hosts, it will be more than the whims of a girl. The spirits that hamper the soul of the King cannot be children and girls.
SAUL: It may be so. Yet though I wrestle, the spirit of the Deep will not come to me. And the wound is greater than a wound in battle, bleeding inwardly. I am a strange man unto myself.
DAVID: Yet Saul is King, comely in his pride, and a great leader in battle. His *deeds* cry unto the whirlwind and are heard. Why should Saul wrestle with the Lord? Saul speaks in actions, and in the time of action the spirit of God comes upon him, and he is King in the sight of all men.
SAUL: It is even so. Yet my soul does not cease to ache, like the soul of a scorned woman, because the Lord will not descend upon me and give me peace in strength.
DAVID: Who is strong like Saul, in Israel?
SAUL: Yet his strength is as a drunken man's—great with despair.
DAVID: Nay, O King! These are fancies. How can my lord speak of despair, when victory is with him, and the light is on his brow in the sight of all Israel!
SAUL: Can I so deceive myself?
DAVID: Surely the King deceives himself.
JONATHAN: Surely, Father, it is a strange self-deception you put on yourself.
SAUL: Can it be so? Yet if so, why does Samuel visit me no more, and withhold his blessing? And why do I feel the ache in me, and the void, where the Full should be? I cannot get at the Lord.

MICHAL: May I speak, my Father?

SAUL: Yea!

MICHAL: Why not laugh as you used to laugh, Father, and throw the spear in sport, at a mark, not grip it in anger? Saul is beautiful among men, to make women weep for joy if he smile at them. Yet his face is heavy with a frown.

SAUL: Why should I smile at thee, witch?

MICHAL: To gladden me, Father. For I am no witch.

SAUL: And when dost thou need gladdening, say?

MICHAL: Now, Father, even here!

SAUL: Thy sorrows are deep, I warrant me.

[*Touches her cheek with his fingers.*]

MICHAL: Yea! Did not this strange young man—indeed he is but a boy—find me chidden and disgraced and in tears before the King?

SAUL: And what then?

MICHAL: Who is this boy from the sheepfolds of Bethlehem, that he should think lightly of the King's daughter in Gilgal?

DAVID: Nay! What man could think lightly of Michal, the daughter of Saul? Her eyes are like the stars shining through a tree at midnight.

MICHAL: Why through a tree?

SAUL [*laughing suddenly*]: Thou bird of the pert whistle! Run! Run, quail! Get thee among the maidens! Thou hast piped long enough before the men.

MICHAL: Even if I run my thoughts run with me.

SAUL: What thoughts, bird of mischief?

MICHAL: That this boy, ruddy with the shepherd's sun, has seen my tears and my disgrace.

DAVID: Surely the tears of Michal are like falling stars in the lonely midnight.

MICHAL: Why, again, in the night?

SAUL [*laughing aloud*]: Be gone! Be gone! No more! [*Exit* MICHAL.]

SAUL: She is a chick of the King's nest! Think not of her, David!

DAVID: But she is pleasant to think of.

SAUL: Even when she mocks thee?

DAVID: Very pleasant.

SAUL: The young men flee from a mocking woman.

DAVID: Not when the voice is sweet.

SAUL: Is Michal's voice sweet? To me at times it is snarling and bad in my ears.

DAVID: That is only when the harp-strings of the King's ears are unstrung.

SAUL: It may be. Yet I think I am cursed in my women-folk. Was not the mother of Jonathan a thorn in my heart? What dost thou prescribe for a thorn in the heart, young wiseling?

DAVID: Pluck it out, O King, and throw it aside, and it is forgotten.

SAUL: But is it easy to pluck out a rancorous woman from the heart?

DAVID: I have no certain knowledge. Yet it should not be hard, I think.

SAUL: How?

DAVID: A man asks in his heart: *Lord, Who fannest the fire of my soul into strength, does the woman cast fuel on the Lord's fire within me, or does she cast wet sand?* Then if the Lord says: *She casts wet sand;* she departs for ever from a man's presence, and a man will go nigh unto her no more, because she seeks to quench the proper fire which is within him.

SAUL: Thou art wiser than if thou hadst been many times wived. Thou art a cocksure stripling.

DAVID: My brothers say of me, I am a cocksure malapert. Yet I do not wish to be! Why am I so, my lord?

SAUL [*laughing*]: It must be the Lord made thee so.

DAVID: My brother has struck me in the face, before now, for words in which I saw no harm.

SAUL [*laughing*]: Didst see the harm afterwards?

DAVID: Not I. I had a bruised mouth, and that was harm enough. But I thought still the words were wise.

SAUL [*laughing*]: Dost think so even yet?

DAVID: Yea, they were wise words. But unwisely spoken.

SAUL [*laughing heartily*]: The Lord sends the wisdom, and leaves thee to spend it! You offer a tit-bit to a wolf, and he takes your fingers as well.

DAVID: I shall learn in the King's household.

SAUL: Among the wolves?

DAVID: Nay, the lion is nobler than the wolf.

SAUL: He will not grudge thee thy callow wisdom.—I go to speak with Abner.

DAVID: Can I serve the King in anything?

SAUL: Not now.

    [*Exit.*]

DAVID: He has gone in good humour.

JONATHAN: We found him in an evil one.

DAVID: Evil spirits out of the earth possess him, and laughter from a maiden sounds to him as the voice of a hyena sounds to a wounded man stricken in the feet.

JONATHAN: It is so. He rails at his daughter, and at the mother who bore me, till my heart swells with anger. Yet he was not always so. Why is it?

DAVID: He has lost the Lord, he says.

JONATHAN: But how? Have I lost the Lord, too?

DAVID: Nay! You are good.

JONATHAN: I wish I knew how my father had lost the Lord.—You David, the Dawn is with you. It is in your face.—Do you wrestle before the Lord?

DAVID: Who am I, that I should wrestle before the Lord? But when I feel the Glory is with me, my heart leaps like a young kid, and bounds in my bosom, and my limbs swell like boughs that put forth buds. —Yet I would not be vainglorious.

JONATHAN: Do you dwell willingly here in Gilgal?

DAVID: I am strange here, and I miss my father, and the hills where the sheep are, in Bethlehem. Yet I comfort myself, turning my soul to the Nameless; and the flame flares up in my heart, and dries my tears, and I am glad.

JONATHAN: And when my father has been bitter and violent, and you go alone in tears, in a strange place —I have seen the tears, and my heart has been sad— then do you yearn for Bethlehem, and your own?

DAVID: I am weak still.—But when I see the stars, and the Lord in darkness alive between them, I am at home, and Bethlehem or Gilgal is the same to me.

JONATHAN: When I lie alone in camp, and see the stars, I think of my mother, and my father, and Michal, and the home place.—You, the Lord becomes a home to you, wherever you are.

DAVID: It is so. I had not thought of it.

JONATHAN: I fear you would never love man nor woman, nor wife nor child, dearly.

DAVID: Nay! I love my father dearly, and my brothers and my mother.

JONATHAN: But when the Lord enters your soul, father or mother or friend is as nothing to you.

DAVID: Why do you say so?—They are the same. But when the Lord is there, all the branches are hidden in blossom.

JONATHAN: Yea!—I, alas, love man or woman with the heart's tenderness, and even the Lord cannot make me forget.

DAVID: But nor do I forget.—It is as if all caught fire at once, in the flame of the Hope.

JONATHAN: Sometimes I think the Lord takes from me the flame I have. I love my father. And my father lifts the short spear at me, in wild anger, because, he says, the Fire has left him, and I am undutiful.

DAVID: The King is the Lord's anointed. The King has known, as none know, the strong gladness of the Lord's presence in his limbs. And then the pain of wanting the Lord, when He cometh not, passes the pain of a woman moaning for the man she loves, who has abandoned her.

JONATHAN: Yet we love the King. The people look up to him. Abner, the chief captain, is faithful to him unto death. Is this nothing to a man?

DAVID: To a man, it is much. To the Lord's anointed, it is much riches. But to the King whom the Lord hath rejected, even love is a hurt.

JONATHAN: Is my father truly rejected from being King, as Samuel said? And merely that he spared

Agag and a few Amalekite cattle? I would not willingly have drawn the sword on naked Agag.

DAVID: Who knows? I know not.—When a people choose a King, then the will of the people is as God to the King. But when the Lord of All chooses a King, then the King must answer to the Lord of All.

JONATHAN: And the Lord of All required the death of defenceless Agag?

DAVID: Amalek has set his will against the Whirlwind. There are two motions in the world. The will of man for himself, and the desire that moves the Whirlwind. When the two are one, all is well, but when the will of man is against the Whirlwind, all is ill, at last. So all is decreed ill, that is Amalek. And Amalek must die, for he obstructs the desire of the breathing God.

JONATHAN: And my father?

DAVID: He is King, and the Lord's anointed.

JONATHAN: But his will is the will of a man, and he cannot bend it with the Lord's desire?

DAVID: It seems he cannot. Yet I know nothing.

JONATHAN: It grieves me for my father. Why is it you can soothe him? Why cannot I?

DAVID: I know not. It is the Lord.

JONATHAN: And why do I love thee?

DAVID: It is the Lord.

JONATHAN: But do you love me again, David?

DAVID: If a man from the sheep dare love the King's son, then I love Jonathan. But hold it not against me for presumption.

JONATHAN: Of a surety, lovest thou me, David?

DAVID: As the Lord liveth.

JONATHAN: And it shall be well between us, for ever?
DAVID: Thou art the King's son. But as the Lord liveth and keepeth us, it shall be well between me and thee. And I will serve thee.
JONATHAN: Nay, but love my soul.
DAVID: Thy soul is dear to my soul, dear as life.
  [*They embrace silently.*]
JONATHAN: And if my father sends thee away, never forget me.
DAVID: Not while my heart lives, can I forget thee.—But David will easily pass from the mind of the son of the King.
JONATHAN: Ah never! For my heart is sorrowful, with my father, and thou art my comfort. I would thou wert King's son, and I shepherd in Bethlehem.
DAVID: Say not so, lest thine anger rise on me at last, to destroy me.
JONATHAN: Nay, it will not.

CURTAIN

SCENE VI

Yard of SAUL's *house in Gilgal.* MICHAL *with tambourine, singing or talking to herself.*

MICHAL: As for me, I am sad, I am sad, I am sad, and why should I not be sad? All things together want to make me sad. I hate the house when the men are gone to war. All the men are gone out against the Philistine. Gone these many days. And never a victory. No one coming home with spoil, and no occasion to dance. I am sad, I am sad, my life is useless to me. Even when they come, they will not bring David. My father looked pleasantly on him for a while, then sent him away. So are men! Such is a king! Sent him away again! And I know, some day when the Lord has left Saul, he will marry me to some old sheik.—Unless he dies in the war. Anyhow, everybody is gone, and I am dull, dull. They say it is the Lord. But why should the Lord make the house of Saul dreary? As for me, I don't know whether the Lord is with me, or whether He is not with me. How should I know? Why should I care! A woman looks with different eyes into her heart, and, Lord or no Lord, I want what I want. I wish I had a sure charm to call back David, son of Jesse. The spells I have tried were no good. I shall try again with the sand and the bones. [*She puts a little sand, and three small white bones, in her tambourine —mutters and bends—tosses her tambourine softly and drops it on the ground. Kneels and gazes intently.*] Bones, bones, show me the ways in the sand. Sand, lie still, sand lie still and speak. Now then, I see the hills of Judah, where Bethlehem is. But David is not there, he is gone. At least I don't see him. In the sand is a road to Gilgal, by the white crown-bone. But he is not coming this way, that I can see. Where else? Where else? This must be Elah in the sand, where my father is. And there is Shochoh, opposite, where the Philistines are. Ah yes, two hills, and a valley between, with a brook in the bottom. And my father with our men on one slope, the Philistines on the other. Ah yes, that will be my father among our men; at least that is his black tent. But Jonathan is not there. O woe, if Jonathan were killed! My heart is afraid for Jonathan. Though how should I know Jonathan as a speck of sand, anyhow? There is nothing in the sand. I am no wise woman, nor a seeress, even though I would like to be. How dull it is! How dull it is here! How dull it is to be a woman! [*Throws away her tambourine.*] Why do they sit in front of the Philistines without defeating them!

WATCHMAN [*entering from the gate*]: Men are coming, from the host of Saul. They come with a litter.

SOLDIER [*entering*]: The Lord strengthen you.

MICHAL: Who comes? Is it news of victory?

SOLDIER: No, lady! Jonathan is wounded in the knee, and comes home to rest.

MICHAL: Wounded in the knee? And what else?

SOLDIER: How, else?

MICHAL: Oh, slow-witted! What other news? Are the Philistines defeated and slaughtered?
SOLDIER: Nay, they are not.
MICHAL: Then what has happened?
SOLDIER: Naught has happened.
MICHAL: Where is the King? Is all well with him?
SOLDIER: The King is with the host at Elah, and all is well with him.
MICHAL: Then where are the Philistines?
SOLDIER: The Philistines are arranged over against us, on the opposite hill at Shochoh.
MICHAL: And what has happened? Do Israel and the Philistines sing songs to one another?
SOLDIER: Nay! A portion of the men go forth to fight, wellnigh each day. And the champion of the Philistines comes each day to challenge us.
MICHAL: And who answers out of Israel?
SOLDIER: None answers.
MICHAL: None answers! Yea, that is news to hear! Has Israel never a champion? Is my father, the King, sick?
SOLDIER: Many champions have we, forsooth. But we are men. And this Philistine is huge: he is out of the old days, before the Flood. He is a huge giant, whose great voice alone shakes the tents.
MICHAL: And not one man answers his challenge?
SOLDIER: Nay, where shall we find a huge giant among us, to answer him?
MICHAL: If he were a mountain, I would prick him with my needle.
SOLDIER: Yes; and would you might prick the eyeballs of him!

[*Enter litter-bearers with* JONATHAN.]

MICHAL: This is most strange!—Ah, Jonathan, and art thou wounded in the knee?
JONATHAN: Yea!
MICHAL: The Lord be praised it is not in the calf!
JONATHAN: Hush, shrew!
MICHAL: Did the Philistine giant wound thee in the knee, O Jonathan?
JONATHAN: A Philistine wounded me.
MICHAL: But I hear they boast a giant, a champion.
JONATHAN: Yea, verily.
MICHAL: A huge unheard-of giant.
JONATHAN: Huge enough: and heard daily.
MICHAL: What does he say, daily?
JONATHAN: Oh——he asks that we send down a man to fight with him. And if he, the Philistine of Gath, slay our man, then shall all Israel be servant to the Philistines. But if our man slay this Goliath, then the Philistines shall be our servants. And seeing that this giant be so large, no ordinary man can get past his sword to attack him, therefore the King is not willing that the fight be settled between champions, lest we lose our freedom in a moment.
MICHAL: And dare no man go up against this huge one?
JONATHAN: Nay, many dare. And many a man seeks to go. I myself would willingly go. Though I know I should die. But what would I care about dying, if the Philistine died first? Yet I doubt *I* should die first, and Israel be delivered into bondage. Hence the King will accept no champion from our midst. But we shall sally forth in daily companies, and defeat the Philistines at length.
MICHAL: At a great length.
JONATHAN: Hast thou wounds or pain, to find it so?

MICHAL: Yea, the wound of shame, that Israel, challenged, is dumb. Israel has no champion! What wound of shame for the woman!

JONATHAN: Why risk the nation in a fight between champions? We are all champions, and we all fight the Philistine.

MICHAL: Only not this big one.

JONATHAN: In single combat, with the fate of the nation hanging in the issue, no! But if Goliath mingle in the battle ranks, then every man of Benjamin will have at him.

MICHAL: And mingles he not in the battle ranks?

JONATHAN: Ah no! He saves himself for the single combat, for this bawling of the challenge and the rattling of the oversized shield.

MICHAL: Some man should think of a way.

JONATHAN: Think thou! I must rest, and recover, and return to the field of battle.

CURTAIN

SCENE VII

The camp of the Israelites at Elah. In the background, black tents of worsted. Morning. Men assembling in arms, to battle. Much shouting of war-cries—much noise of war-like anticipation. DAVID *entering, carrying a staff.*

DAVID: Is yon the tent of Eliab of Bethlehem?
SOLDIER: The tent of the sons of Jesse.
SHAMMAH [*coming armed from the tent*]: Is not this our brother David? [*Calling.*] Ho! David is here! [*Embracing* DAVID.] And art thou also come to the fight?
ELIAB [*also armed*]: What, David! Hast thou left the sheep to come among the men-at-arms?
[*They embrace.*]
DAVID: My father sent me here to inquire of you, and to bring you bread, and the cheeses for the captain of your thousand. The loaves and the parched corn and the cheeses have I left with the keeper of the victuals. But where is Abinadab?
ELIAB: With the host, where we must form to battle.
[*The men are forming in loose array,* ABINADAB *comes and embraces* DAVID.]
ABINADAB: Hast thou come from Bethlehem? And how is our father, and all the homestead?

DAVID: Yea, all are well. My father sent me with victual, and to see how you fare, and to take your pledge.

ELIAB: The pledge we will give you after the fight. And how fares my young son at home?

CAPTAIN [*calling*]: The thousand of Judah, get you to your hundreds: get you to your places. [*Bustle of men falling into rank.*]

DAVID [*following his brothers*]: Your son was bitten by a hound, but all is well.

ELIAB: What hound, forsooth? And lives the dog yet?

SAUL [*passing*]: Five hundred of Benjamin, lead into the valley!

SOLDIERS: Ah! Ah! The five hundred are moving forth!
[*Loud shouting of* SOLDIERS.]

DAVID: And how goes the fight?

SHAMMAH: Wellah, this way and that, as wind bloweth!

DAVID: The days are many, that you are afield. My father grew uneasy, and could stay no longer. Long days and no news are ill to live, said he.

ELIAB: Tell my father, this is no folding of sheep, out here.

DAVID: And has no weighty blow been struck, on either side?

SOLDIERS [*calling*]: Ha! Ha! The five hundred are near the brook! And behold, the Philistine champion cometh forth from the ranks, to meet them.
[*Hush in the camp.*]

MIGHTY VOICE OF GOLIATH: Ho! Ho, there! Israel! Why are ye come to set your battle array? Am I not a Philistine, and ye servants to Saul? Choose you a man for you, and let him come down to me.

DAVID [*in the hush*]: But who is this?
SOLDIERS: Ha! Ha! The five hundred are fleeing back from him! They are sore afraid.
[*A hush.*]
SHAMMAH: This is Goliath, their champion.
VOICE OF GOLIATH: Ha! ha! Why run ye? Choose you a man for you, and let him come down to me. If he can fight with me, and kill me, then will we be your servants. But if I prevail against him, and kill him, then shall ye be our servants, and serve us. It is fairly said. Choose you a man for you!
DAVID [*in the hush*]: Surely he is a huge man! Goeth no man forth to meet him?
SOLDIER: Have you seen this man! Surely, forty days has he come up to defy Israel. And it shall be, that the man who killeth him, the King will enrich him with great riches, and will give him his daughter, and make his father's house free in Israel.
DAVID: What will the King do to the man that killeth this Philistine and taketh away the reproach from Israel? Will he surely give him his daughter? The daughter of his house in Gilgal?
SOLDIER: Aye, surely he will. And much riches. And make his father's house free in Israel.
DAVID: Who is this uncircumcised Philistine, that he should defy the armies of the living God?
SOLDIERS: Ah! He is what thou seest.
DAVID: As the Lord liveth, there shall be an end to him.
SOLDIERS: Would it were so! But who shall do it?
DAVID: Is the Lord naught in the reckoning? The Lord is with me, and I will do it.
SOLDIERS: Thou? How canst thou kill this great giant?

Scene VII — DAVID

DAVID: I can do it. I will kill him, as the Lord liveth in me, were his name six times Goliath.

SOLDIER: Nay, but how?

DAVID: The Lord will show you how. I, I will kill him.

ELIAB [*coming forward*]: What art thou doing here? Why camest thou hither, and with whom hast thou left those few sheep in the wilderness? I know thy pride, and the naughtiness of thy heart. For thou art come down that thou mightest see the battle.

DAVID: What have I now done? Was I not sent by my father, for a cause?

ELIAB [*turning away in anger*]: Thou didst persuade him, in the vanity of thy mind.

SOLDIER: Shall we say to Saul of thee, that thou art minded to kill the giant?

DAVID: Say so to him. For the Lord is with me.

ANOTHER SOLDIER: Verily, feelest thou in the power to kill this mighty man?

DAVID: Verily! And is it sooth the King will give his daughter to him that slayeth the roaring Philistine?

SOLDIER: Yea, it is sooth, for it is so proclaimed. But tell us how thou wilt come nigh him, to slay him.

DAVID: The Lord will show you.

SOLDIERS: Saul is coming.

SAUL [*approaching*]: Which is this man will go forth against the Philistine?

DAVID: Let no man's heart fail because of the giant, for thy servant will go out and fight with him.

SAUL: Thou? Thou art not able to go against this Philistine to fight with him, for thou art but a youth, and he is a man of war from his youth.

DAVID: Thy servant slew both the lion and the bear; and this uncircumcised Philistine shall be as one of them, seeing he hath defied the armies of the living God.

SAUL: But neither lion nor bear came against thee in greaves of brass nor armed with sword a man's length. How shallst thou fight with this giant in panoply?

DAVID: The Lord that delivered me out of the paw of the lion, and out of the paw of the bear, He will deliver me out of the hand of the Philistine.

SAUL: Thou shalt go. And the Lord be with thee. [*To* ARMOUR-BEARER.] Fetch hither my armour, and another sword. For we will put them on him.
    [*Exit* ARMOUR-BEARER.]

DAVID: Shall thy servant go in armour clad?

SAUL: How else canst thou keep thy life?

VOICE OF GOLIATH: Ho! men of Saul! Is there no man among you, to answer when a fighter calls? Are you all maidens, combing your hair? Where is Saul, the slayer of foemen? Is he crying like a quail to his God? Call to Baal, and call to Astaroth, for the God of Israel is a pigeon in a box.

DAVID: Ha! Lord God! Deliver him into my hand this day!

SAUL: Yea! [*Enter* ARMOUR-BEARER.] Put the coat of proof upon him, and the helmet of brass.
    [*They put the armour of the* KING *on* DAVID.]

DAVID: I am not used to it.

SAUL [*unbuckling his sword*]: Take thou my sword.

DAVID [*girding it on*]: Thy servant hath honour beyond his lot. Lo! I am strange in this array! The Lord hath not intended it for me.
    [*Takes shield.*]

SAUL: Now thou art ready. A man shall bear thy shield.

DAVID: Then let me go. But let me assay this sword and battle harness that is on me. [*Sets forth. Tries his sword; goes a little way. Turns suddenly back.*] I cannot go with these, for I have not proved them.
  [*Drops his shield. Hastily unbuckles sword, and gives it to* SAUL. *Unfastens the helmet. The* ARMOUR-BEARER *disarms* DAVID.]
SAUL: Then thou goest not! Uncovered thou canst not go.
DAVID: As the Lord liveth, I will go with naught but God upon me.
VOICE OF GOLIATH: The God of Israel is a blue pigeon in a box, and the men of Israel are quails in the net of the Philistine. Baal is laughing aloud, and Astarte smiles behind her sleeve, for Israel is no more than worms in a dung-hill.
DAVID: I shall go. Sound the trumpet!
  [*He picks up his staff, recrosses hastily to the back of the stage, downwards as to a valley. Stoops in the distance: meanwhile trumpet sounds, and the voice of the* HERALD *is heard, crying.*]
HERALD: Come down, Goliath! Come forward, Philistine! For Israel sendeth a champion against thee.
  [*Noise of shouting in both camps.*]
SHAMMAH: See, David is picking smooth stones from the brook bed.
ABINADAB: He has put them in his leather pouch, and taken his sling in his hand. Surely he will go after the Philistine as after a wolf.
SAUL: The Philistine cometh down, with his shield-bearer before him.—Yea, but the youth is naked and unafraid.
VOICE OF GOLIATH: Where art thou, champion of

Israel? I see thee not. Hast thou already perished of
thy dread?
VOICE OF DAVID [*small*]: Yea, I am coming.
VOICE OF GOLIATH: Thou!
SAUL: How he disdains the youth! If we have lost all
on this throw!
VOICE OF GOLIATH: Am I a dog, that thou comest to
me with staves? Now shall Astaroth slay thee with
spittle, and Baal shall break thy bones with a loud
laugh.
VOICE OF DAVID: Thou comest to me with a sword, and
with a spear, and with a shield: but I come to thee
in the name of the Lord of Hosts, the God of the
armies of Israel, Whom thou hast defied.
VOICE OF GOLIATH: Come! Ha-ha! Come to me, and I
will give thy flesh to the fowls of the air, and to
the wild beasts of the hills.

[*Meanwhile the bystanders*, SHAMMAH, ABIN-
ADAB, SOLDIERS, *all save the* ARMOUR-BEARER *and*
SAUL, *have been running to the far background,
to look closer.*]

VOICE OF DAVID: This day will the Lord deliver thee
into my hand; and I will smite thee, and take thy
head from thee.
VOICE OF GOLIATH: Ha! Ha! Canst thou chirp? Come
over, thou egg, that they see me swallow thee.

[*Loud yelling from Philistines.*]

VOICE OF DAVID: I will give the carcass of the host of
the Philistines this day to the fowls of the air, and
to the beasts of the earth. That all the earth may
know there is a God in Israel.

[*Loud yelling of Israel.*]

VOICE OF GOLIATH: Come, thou whistling bird! Come! Seest thou this sword?

[*Loud yelling of Philistines.*]

VOICE OF DAVID: Yea! and all this people shall know that the Lord saveth not with sword and spear: for the battle is the Lord's, and He will deliver you into our hands.

[*Great defiance heard in Israel.*]

VOICE OF GOLIATH: Must we die of thy talking? And wilt thou not come forth? Then must I fetch thee. . . .

[*Tumult in Philistia.*]

ARMOUR-BEARER: The Philistine is hastening down!—Oh, and behold, the youth is running at him fast! Ha-a-a!

[ARMOUR-BEARER *rushes away, leaving* SAUL *alone.*]

SAUL [*in a pause*]: Ah! Ah!—Lord, my Lord!—Is he down? [*Great shouting heard—men running.*] What? Yea, the Philistine has fallen! The boy but slang a stone at him! It is the Lord! Nay, he riseth not!—Ah God! was it so easy a thing? Why had I not done it! See, see, Saul, see, thou King of Israel, see this nameless boy who hath run upon the fallen Philistine, and seized his sword from his hand, and stands upon his body hewing at the neck of the giant! Ah, sight for the King of Israel, who stands alone, in safety, far off, and watches this thing done for him! Yea, they may shout! It is not for me. It is for that boy, whom I know not. How should I know him, with his young beard on his lip! It is a hard thing to hack off the head of such a giant, and he cannot find the neck joint. I see him stooping! [*A great wild shout is heard.*] Ah! Even so! Even so!

ABNER [*entering running*]: The youth has slain the Philistine with a stone from a sling, and even now has hewn his head loose, and is holding it up before the armies.

SAUL: Even so!

ABNER: Yea! He stands upon the body of that which was Goliath, and holds up the head to Israel! The Lord has prevailed.

[*Loud shouting.*]

SOLDIERS [*running past*]: The host of the Philistines is in flight! After them! After them!

ABNER: Shall we not pursue? Will not the King lead the pursuit? Lo! they flee in abandon, flinging away their spears in their haste.

SAUL: This needs no leader. Any man can strike in the back of a running enemy. What of the youth?

ABNER: He hath stripped the Philistine of his gear. Yea, I can see the body of the giant naked in blood upon the ground.

SAUL: Who is this youth? Whose son is he?

ABNER: As thy soul liveth, O King, I cannot tell.

SAUL: Enquire thou whose son the stripling is.

ABNER: He is coming towards the brook. I will bring him hither.

[*Exit.*]

SAUL: Yea, he is coming! And alone up the slope, for the men have gone like hounds after the Philistine, and to the stripping of the tents. Yea, as bees swarm in upon the sweetmeats, when the window is opened. This is a day to make songs for. But not in the name of Saul. Whom will the maidens sing to? To him yonder, coming up the hill slowly, with the swinging head, and the bright brass armour of the Philistine. To that ruddy-faced fair youth, with a young beard on his mouth. It seems I should know him, if I would. Yea, I shall know him in my hour. Ah the blithe thing! Ah the blithe boy! Ah God! God! was I not blithe? Where is it gone? Yea, where! Blitheness in a man is the Lord in his body. Nay, boy, boy! I would not envy thee the head of the Philistine. Nay, I would not envy thee the Kingdom itself. But the blitheness of thy body, that is thy Lord in thee, I envy it thee with a sore envy. For once my body too was blithe. But it hath left me. It hath left me. Not because I am old. And were I ancient as Samuel is, I could still have the alertness of God in me, and the blithe bearing of the living God upon me. I have lost the best. I had it, and have let it go. Ha! whither is he going? He turns aside, among the tents. Aha! Aha! So it is. Among the tents of Judah, and to the booth of the Bethlehemite! So, he has gone in to lay down his spoil, the helmet of brass, and the greaves of brass, the coat, the great sword, and the shirt fringed with scarlet. Lay them by, they are thine. Yea, they are thine, lay them in thy tent. No need to bring them unto the King. They are no king's spoil. Yea, lead him hither, Abner! Lead him hither! He is bringing the head in his hand. Oh yes, the champion, the victor! He is bringing the head in his hand, to swing it under the nose of the King. But the sword, the great sword, and the greaves of brass and the body-spoil he has e'en laid by in his own tent, where no man may lay hand on it. Oh! it is a shrewd youth,

and a canny youth, cunning as the Lord makes them.
   [*Enter* DAVID, *with head of* GOLIATH—*and*
   ABNER.]
SAUL: So! Comest thou again?
DAVID: Even so! To lay the head of thine enemy before thee, O King!
SAUL: Whose son art thou, thou young man?
DAVID: I am the son of thy servant Jesse the Bethlehemite.
SAUL: Art thou so! Ay, thou art David! And brother to Eliab, and Abinadab, and Shammah, three men of war!—Thou hast put cunning in thy skill, and slain thine enemy as he were a hare among the bushes.
ABNER: See! The place where the stone sunk in, in the side of the forehead bone! It lies still there, the stone of David.
SAUL: Yea, that was death without weapons meeting, indeed.
ABNER: Surely the Lord was in that round stone, that digged the pit in Goliath's head-bone!
DAVID: Except the Lord had been with me, I had not done it.
SOLDIERS [*standing round*]: Yea, the Lord sped the hand of David. The Lord is with this young man.
SAUL: Praise we must give to the Lord, and to David the promised reward. Seekest thou thy reward at the King's hand, thou young man?
DAVID: It is as the King willeth. Yet what should the reward be?
SAUL: Hast thou not heard it proclaimed?
DAVID: Nay, I arrived but in the dawn, with provender from my father to my brethren.

Scene VII DAVID 55

SAUL: Didst thou not set forth even now against the Philistine, hoping big for the reward?

DAVID: Not so, O King. But the Lord moved me to go, to take off the shame and the reproach from the army of the living God.

SAUL: Thou hast done well! Yet claimest thou thy reward?

DAVID: Shall I not hear from the King's mouth, what the reward should be?

SAUL: How was it said, Abner? Recallest thou?

ABNER: Yea, O King! Riches and the King's daughter, and freedom for his father's house, to the man that should slay Goliath in the single combat.

SAUL: Single-handed hath David slain Goliath, indeed! Even without any combat at all. But how likest thou thy reward, thou young man?

DAVID: Were it mine, O King, I should rejoice for my father's sake, and fall to the ground beneath the honour put upon me, being son-in-law to the King.

SAUL: Even so! Now thou shalt stay with me, and live in my house, and return no more to thy father's house. And all shall be done to thee, as was said.— For surely thou hast brought much honour upon Israel. And we will make much of thee. For thou art champion of Israel in the sight of all the people. And thou shalt sit at the King's right hand, that all men may delight in thee. Yet, since thou art young, and fresh from the sheepfold, we will not hasten thee to thy confusion. But thou shalt dwell as a son among us, and rise in degree as a son rises, sitting at the King's meat. And behold, my elder daughter Merab, her will I give thee to wife. Only be thou valiant for me, and fight the Lord's battles.

DAVID: Let but thy servant serve thee, O King, in the sight of the Lord. And Saul will take the head of this Philistine, to put it on a pole?

SAUL: Nay! Thou thyself shalt bring it before the people, in Jerusalem of Judah.

CURTAIN

SCENE VIII

The KING's *tent at Elah: a square tent of dark worsted, with the wide front open. Heaps of panoply and spoil without. Within, in the public part of the tent,* SAUL, *with* DAVID *on his right hand,* JONATHAN *on his left, and sitting around, the* CAPTAINS *of the armies of Israel.*

SAUL: We have numbered the armies in tens, in hundreds, and in thousands. And now are all men returned from pursuing after the Philistine, and the spoil is all brought in. And the wounded of the Philistine have fallen by the way, even to the valley of Ekron and the gates of Gath, their dead are more than their living. Yet are their princes within the land, holding on to strong places. Therefore we will rejoice not yet, nor go home to the feasting. But while his heart is sunk low, we will follow up the Philistine in every place where he holds out. Is it sooth?
CAPTAIN: It is good, O King.
ABNER: The blow that was struck with a pebble, we will follow up with swords and spears, till in the Lord's name not one uncircumcised remains in the land.
CAPTAIN: It is good! It is good!
   [*They strike their shields.*]
SAUL [*presenting* DAVID]: This is David, that slew Goliath the Philistine, and delivered Israel from re-

proach. Sits not David high in the heart of every man in Israel, this day?

CAPTAINS: Yea! David! David!
  [*Striking shields.*]

SAUL: Who is first among the men of war this day? Is it not David, my son David?

CAPTAINS: David! David! It is David!

SAUL: Yea, Captains! Your King is but captain of the captains! Whom shall we set over the men of war this day? Shall it not be David? This time, shall not David lead the hosts? Is he not the first against the Philistine? Yea, in this foray of triumph and this campaign of victory, should any man lead but David?

CAPTAINS: It is good! David shall command, till we return home this time from smiting the Philistine.
  [*They clash shields with martial noise.*]

SAUL [*to* DAVID]: Hearest thou, David, son of my delight?

DAVID: O King, I am no leader of men of war. I have no skill in arts of battle. Honour me not to my confusion.

SAUL: Nay, this time shalt thou take the charge. For in *this* fight art thou the first man among the men of war in Israel. Answer, Captains! Is it not so?

CAPTAINS: Verily! This time we will have David.

ABNER: Verily, save David lead us, we will not go.
  [*The* CAPTAINS *rise, and lift locked shields before* DAVID *as if to raise him up.*]

SAUL: If we go not now, we lose the golden hour. The choice is upon thee, David.

DAVID: Thy servant will do according to thy will, O King, and according to the will of Abner, and of the Captains. [*He rises before the* CAPTAINS.] But I am young, and not brought up to war. And the Captains and the strong men will laugh at me, seeing my inexperience and my presumption.

ABNER: Nay! No man shall find occasion to laugh at thee, for the fight is in thee as in a young eagle. Leading to war shalt thou learn war.

DAVID: It is as the King and the Captains shall bid me.

SAUL [*rising*]: We will make ready, and send out the news through the camp: *In this is David our leader!* Then David shall choose his men, and go forth. He shall give his orders, and the Captains shall march at his bidding. David, the day is thine!

[*Salutes. The* CAPTAINS *again salute* DAVID *with spear on shield, then they go out.*]

CAPTAINS: To thee, David!

[*Exeunt.*]

DAVID [*to* JONATHAN]: How shall I bring this to a pass?

JONATHAN: Thy soul will not fail thee. Thou art the young lion of Judah, thou art the young eagle of the Lord. O David, is it well between me and thee, and hast thou verily not forgotten me?

DAVID: Verily, thou hast not left my soul. But how shall I go before these men?

JONATHAN: We have sworn a covenant, is it not between us? Wilt thou not swear with me, that our souls shall be as brothers, closer even than the blood? O David, my heart hath no peace save all be well between thy soul and mine, and thy blood and mine.

DAVID: As the Lord liveth, the soul of Jonathan is dearer to me than a brother's.—O brother, if I were but come out of this pass, and we might live before the Lord, together!

JONATHAN: What fearest thou then?
DAVID: In the Lord, I fear nothing. But before the faces of men, my heart misgives me.
JONATHAN: Sittest thou not high in the hearts of Israel?
DAVID: Yea, but who am I, to be suddenly lifted up! Will they not throw me as suddenly down?
JONATHAN: Who would throw thee down, that art strong as a young eagle, and subtle as the leopard?
DAVID: I will rest in the Lord.
JONATHAN: And in me wilt thou not trust?
DAVID: I will trust thee, Jonathan, and cleave to thee till the sun sets on me. Thou art good to me as man never before was good to me, and I have not deserved it. Say thou wilt not repent of thy kindness towards me!
JONATHAN: O brother, give me the oath, that naught shall sunder our souls, for ever.
DAVID: As the Lord liveth, my soul shall not part for ever from the soul of my brother Jonathan; but shall go with him up the steeps of heaven, or down the sides of the pit. And between his house and my house the covenant shall be everlasting. For as the hearts of men are made on earth, the heart of Jonathan is gentlest and most great.
JONATHAN: The covenant is between us.
 [*Covers his face.*]
DAVID [*after a pause*]: But how shall I go before these captains, O my brother? Comest thou not with me? Wilt thou not stand by me? Oh, come!
JONATHAN: I am limping still in the knee, and how shall I lead a foray? But thou art mine and I am

thine. And I will clothe thee in my clothes, and give thee my sword and my bow, and so shall my spirit be added to thy spirit, and thou shalt be as the King's son and the eagle of the Lord, in the eyes of the people.

[*Takes off striped coat, or wide-sleeved tunic.*]

DAVID: But can I do this thing?

JONATHAN: Yea! That all men know thou art as the King's son in the world. For the eagle hath gold in his feathers and the young lion is bright. So shall David be seen in Israel.

[DAVID *slowly pulls off his loose robe, a herdsman's tunic cut off at the knee.* JONATHAN *takes off his sleeveless shirt, and is seen in his leather loin-strap. From his upper arm he takes a metal bracelet.*]

JONATHAN: Even all my garments thou shalt take, even the armlet that should not leave me till I die. And thou shalt wear it for ever. And thy garments will I take upon me, so the honour shall be mine.

[DAVID *pulls off his shirt, and is seen in the leather loin-strap,* JONATHAN *puts his bracelet on* DAVID's *arm, then his own shirt over* DAVID's *head, and holds up his coloured robe.* DAVID *robed,* JONATHAN *brings him a coloured head-kerchief and girdle, then his sword and his bow and quiver and shoes.* JONATHAN *puts on* DAVID's *clothes.*]

DAVID: How do I appear?

JONATHAN: Even as the eagle in his own plumage. It is said, David, that thou art anointed of Samuel, before the Lord. Is it so?

DAVID: Yea.
JONATHAN: Thou hast the sun within thee, who shall deny thee?
DAVID: Why speakest thou sadly, Jonathan, brother?
JONATHAN: Lest thou go beyond me, and be lost to me.
DAVID: Lord! Lord! Let not my soul part from the soul of Jonathan for ever, for all that man can be to man on earth, is he to me.
JONATHAN: Would I could give thee more!
SAUL [*entering*]: Yea! And which now is the King's son, and which the shepherd?
DAVID: Thy son would have it so, O King.
JONATHAN: It is well, Father! Shall not the leader shine forth?
SAUL: Even so. And the young King-bird shall moult his feathers in the same hour.
JONATHAN: The robe of David honours the shoulders of Jonathan.
SAUL: Art thou ready, thou brave young man?
DAVID: I am ready, O King.
SAUL: The host is in array, awaiting thy coming.
DAVID: I will come where the King leads me.
SAUL [*to* JONATHAN]: Put another robe upon thee, ere thou come forth.
JONATHAN: I will not come forth. [*Turns abruptly.*]
 [DAVID *follows* SAUL *from the tent—loud shouting of the army.*]
JONATHAN [*alone*]: If the Lord hath anointed him for the kingdom, Jonathan will not quarrel with the Lord. My father knoweth. Yet Saul will strain against God. The Lord hath not revealed Himself unto me: save that once I saw the glisten in my

father that now I see in David. My life belongs to my father, but my soul is David's. I cannot help it. The Lord sees fit to split me between King and King-to-be, and already I am torn asunder as between two wild horses straining opposite ways. Yet my blood is my father's. And my soul is David's. And the right hand and the left hand are strangers on me.

CURTAIN

SCENE IX

Outside the courtyard of SAUL's *house in Gilgal. Doorway of courtyard seen open.* MAIDENS *running forth with instruments of music. Men-servants gazing into the distance. People waiting.*

MAIDENS: Lu-lu-a-li-lu-lu-lu! Lu-lu-lu-li-a-li-lu-lu!
A-li-lu-lu-lu-a-li-lu! Lu-al-li-lu! Lu-al-li-lu-a!
MERAB: Out of Judah Saul comes in!
MICHAL: David slew the Philistine.
MERAB AND HER MAIDENS: Out of Judah Sauls comes in!
MICHAL AND HER MAIDS: David slew the Philistine.
ALL [*repeat several times*]: A-li-lu-lu! A-li-lu-lu-lu!
Lu! lu! lu! lu! li! lu! lu! a! li! lu! lu! lu! lu!
MERAB: All the Philistine has fled.
MICHAL: By the roadside fell their dead.
MERAB: Wounded fell down in the path.
MICHAL: Beyond Ekron unto Gath.
MERAB AND MAIDENS: All the Philistine has fled.
MICHAL AND MAIDENS: By the roadside fell their dead.
MERAB AND MAIDENS: Wounded fell down in the path.
MICHAL AND MAIDENS: Beyond Ekron unto Gath.
ALL [*repeat continuously*]: Lu-li-lu-lu-lu! Lu-lu-li-a-lu-lu! Li-a-li-lu-lu-lu? Lu! Lu! Lu! A! li! Lu! Lu! Lu! Lu! Li! A! Lu! Lu! Li! Lu! A! Li! Lu! Lu! Lu! Lu! u!

MERAB: Saul in thousands slew their men!
MICHAL: David slew his thousands ten!
MERAB AND MAIDENS: Saul in thousands slew their men!
MICHAL AND MAIDENS: David slew his thousands ten! Oh! Lu! Lu! Lu! Lu! Lu! Lu! A! Li! Lu! Lu! Lu!
ALL: Lu! Lu! Lu! Li! Lu! Lu! Lu!—A-li-lu-lu-a-li-lu-lu! Lu-a-li-lu-lu-lu! Lu-lu-lu!
MERAB: Out of Judah Saul comes in.
MICHAL: David slew the Philistine.
MERAB AND MAIDENS: Out of Judah Saul comes in.
MICHAL AND MAIDENS: David slew the Philistine.
ALL: Lu-li-lu-lu-lu-li-lu! Lu-lu-a-li-lu-lu-lu!

[*They continue the repetition of the simple rhymes, as* SAUL *draws near, followed by* DAVID, JONATHAN, ABNER *and the armed men. The* MAIDENS *keep up the singing, all the time dancing;* MERAB *with her* MAIDENS *on one side of the men,* MICHAL *and her* MAIDENS *on the other, singing loudly back and forth all the time. The men pass slowly into the gate, without response. The* MAIDENS *run peering at the spoil the servant-men are carrying in. All pass in at the gate.*]

CURTAIN

SCENE X

Courtyard of SAUL'S *house in Gilgal. Confusion of people and men just come in—*MAIDENS *still singing outside.*

ABNER: The King is returned to his own house once more full of victory. When shall we slay the sacrifice?

SAUL: To-night I will slay a bull calf for my house, and an ox will I sacrifice for my household. And for the men will we slay oxen and sheep and goats.

ABNER: Yea! For this is a great day before the Lord in Israel! And we will sprinkle the spoil with the sacrifice.

SAUL: Hast thou heard the song of women? Nay, hearest thou? Hark!

[*In the distance is heard the singing.*]

MERAB: *Saul in thousands slew his men.*

MICHAL: *David slew his thousands ten.*

ALL: *Lu-lu-lu-li-lu-lu-a! A li-lu-lu-a-li-lu!*

ABNER: Ay!

SAUL: May such mouths be bruised!

ABNER: Nay! Nay! King Saul! In this hour!

SAUL: In this instant! They have ascribed to David ten thousands, and to me they have ascribed but thousands. And what can he have more, but the Kingdom?

ABNER: Nay, nay, O Saul! It is but the light words of women. Ay, let them sing! For as vain women they fancy naught but that head of Goliath, with the round stone sunken in. But the King is King.

SAUL: Shall that shepherd oust me, even from the mouths of the maidens?

ABNER: Nay, this is folly, and less than kingly.

MICHAL [*followed by* MERAB—*running round the* KING *with their tambourines*]: Lu-li-lu-lu-a-li-lu! A-li-lu-lu-a-li-lu-lu-lu!

SAUL: Away!

MERAB AND MICHAL: Lu-lu-lu-lu! Saul, the King! Lu-lu-lu-lu-al-li-lu-lu! Saul! Saul! Lu-lu-lu! Saul! Saul! Lu-lulu!

SAUL: Peace, I say!

[*Exit, passing into house.*]

MERAB AND MICHAL: Jonathan and David. Lu-lu-lu! Here they come, the friendly two! Lu-lu-lu-lu-a-li-lu! Lu-lu-a-li-lu-lu-lu!

MERAB: Jonathan is kingly bred.

MICHAL: David took Goliath's head.

BOTH: Jonathan and David! Lu-lu-lu!—a! Here they come the loving two-a!

MICHAL [*to* DAVID]: Where is the giant's head?

DAVID: It is in Jerusalem of Judah, O Maiden.

MICHAL: Why did you not bring it here, that we might see it?

DAVID: I am of Judah, and they would have it there.

MICHAL: But Saul is King, and could have it where he would.

DAVID: Saul would leave it in Jerusalem.

MICHAL: And the armour, and the greaves of brass, and the shield, and the sword? The coat of brass

that weighs five thousand shekels. Where are these?
I want to see them, O David!

DAVID: The armour is in my father's house, and in
Jerusalem. The sword lies before the Lord in Ramah, with Samuel, O Maiden!

MICHAL: Why take it to Samuel? Do you not know my
name, O David!

DAVID: You are Michal.

MICHAL: I am she. And this is Merab! Look at him,
Merab, and see if you like him. Is it true, O my
brother Jonathan, that the King will give Merab his
daughter to the slayer of the Philistine?

JONATHAN: He hath said so.

MICHAL: To us he has not said one word. O Merab!
Look at thy man! How likest thou him?

MERAB: I will not look at him yet.

MICHAL: Oh, thou! Thou hast spied out every hair in
his beard. Is he not fox-red? I think the beard of a
man should be raven-black. O Merab, thy David is
very ruddy.

MERAB: Nay! He is not yet mine, nor I his.

MICHAL: Thou wouldst it were so! Aiee! Thou art
hasty and beforehand with the red youth! Shame on
thee, that art a King's daughter.

MERAB: Nay, now, I have said naught.

MICHAL: Thou shouldst have said somewhat, to cover
thy unmaidenly longing.—O David, this Merab
sighs in her soul for you. How like you her?

DAVID: She is fair and a modest maiden.

MICHAL: As am not I! Oh, but I am Saul's very daughter, and a hawk that soars king high. And what has
David brought, to lay before Merab?

DAVID: All I have is laid before the King.
MICHAL: But naught of the Philistine Goliath! All that spoil you took home to your father's house, as the fox brings his prey to his own hole. Ah, David, the wary one!
MERAB: It was his own! Where should he take it, but to his father's house!
MICHAL: Is not the King his father! Why should he not bring it here? Is Merab not worth the bride-money?
JONATHAN: Oh, peace! Thou art all mischief, Michal, Thou shouldst be married to a Philistine, for his undoing.
MICHAL: Ayeee! This David has come back to trouble us! Why didst not *thou* slay the Philistine, Jonathan?
JONATHAN: Peace! Let us go in, David! These maidens are too forward. My father did never succeed in ruling his household of women.
MICHAL: Ayee! His household of women! Thou, Jonathan! Go in, David! They shall not put poison in your meat.
 [*As* DAVID *and* JONATHAN *depart she sings:*]
 Empty-handed David came!
 Merab saw him full of shame!
 Lu-lu-lu-lu-lu-li-lu! A-li-lu-a! A-li-lu!
 Empty-handed David came!
 Merab saw him full of shame!
 A-li-lu-lu! A-li-lu-li! Li-lu-li-lu-a!
[*To* MERAB.] So he has come!
MERAB: Even so! Yet his brow says: *Have a care!*
MICHAL: Have a care, Merab! Have a care, David! Have a care, Michal! Have a care, Jonathan! Have

a care, King Saul! I do not like his brow, it is too studied.

MERAB: Nay, it is manly, and grave.

MICHAL: Ayee! Ayee! He did not laugh. He did not once laugh. It will not be well, Merab.

MERAB: What will not be well?

MICHAL: The King will not give thee to him.

MERAB: But the King hath spoken.

MICHAL: I have read the brow of Saul, and it was black. I have looked at David's brow, and it was heavy and secret. The King will not give thee to David, Merab. I know it, I know it.

MERAB: A King should keep his word!

MICHAL: What! Art thou hot with anger against thy father, lest he give thee not to this shepherd boy! David hath cast a spell on Merab! The ruddy herdsman out of Judah has thrown a net over the King's daughter! Oh, poor quail! poor partridge!

MERAB: I am not caught! I am not!

MICHAL: Thou art caught! And not by some chieftain, nor by some owner of great herds. But by a sheep-tending boy! Oh, fie!

MERAB: Nay, I do not want him.

MICHAL: Yea, thou dost. And if some man of great substance came, and my father would give thee to him, thou wouldst cry: *Nay! Nay! Nay! I am David's!*

MERAB: Never would I cry this that thou sayest. For I am not his.—And am I not first daughter of the King!

MICHAL: Thou waitest and pantest after that red David. And he will climb high in the sight of Israel, upon the mound of Merab. I tell thee, he is a climber who would climb above our heads.

MERAB: Above my head he shall not climb.
MICHAL: Empty-handed David came!
         Merab saw him full of shame!
      Lu-li-lu-li! Lu-li-lu-lu-lu-li! A-li-lu-lu!

CURTAIN

SCENE XI

Room in KING's *house at Gilgal. Bare adobe room, mats on the floor.* SAUL, ABNER *and* ADRIEL *reclining around a little open hearth.*

SAUL: And how is the slayer of Goliath looked upon, in Gilgal?
ABNER: Yea! he is a wise young man, he brings no disfavour upon himself.
SAUL: May Baal finish him! And how looks he on the King's daughter? Does he eye Merab as a fox eyes a young lamb?
ABNER: Nay, he is wise, a young man full of discretion, watching well his steps.
SAUL: Ay is he! Smooth-faced and soft-footed, as Joseph in the house of Pharaoh! I tell you, I like not this weasel.
ABNER: Nay, he is no enemy of the King. His eyes are clear, with the light of the Lord God. But he is alone and shy, as a rude young shepherd.
SAUL: Thou art his uncle, surely. I tell you, I will send him back to Bethlehem, to the sheep-cotes.
ABNER: He is grown beyond the sheep-cotes, O King! And wilt thou send him back into Judah, while the giant's head still blackens above the gates of Jerusalem, and David is darling of all Judea, in the hearts of the men of Judah! Better keep him here, where the King alone can honour him.

SAUL: I know him! Should I send him away, he will have them name him King in Judah, and Samuel will give testimony. Yea, when he carried the sword of the giant before Samuel in Ramah, did not Samuel bless him in the sight of all men, saying: Thou art chosen of the Lord out of Israel!

ABNER: If it be so, O King, we cannot put back the sun in heaven. Yet is David faithful servant to the King, and full of love for Jonathan. I find in him no presumption.

SAUL: My household is against me. Ah, this is the curse upon me! My children love my chief enemy, him who hath supplanted me before the Lord. Yea, my children pay court to David, and my daughters languish for him. But he shall not rise upon me. I say he shall not! Nor shall he marry my elder daughter Merab. Wellah, and he shall not.

ABNER: Yet Saul has given his word.

SAUL: And Saul shall take it back. What man should keep his word with a supplanter? Abner, have we not appointed him captain over a thousand? Captain over a thousand in the army of Saul shall he be. Oh yes! And to-morrow I will say to him, I will even say it again: *Behold Merab, my elder daughter, her will I give thee to wife: only be thou valiant for me, and fight the Lord's battles.* And then he shall go forth with his thousand again, quickly, against the Philistine. Let not my hand be upon him, but let the hand of the Philistine be upon him.

ABNER: But if the Lord be with him, and he fall not, but come back once more with spoil, wilt thou then withhold the hand of thy daughter Merab from him?

SAUL: He shall not have her! Nay, I know not. When

the day comes that he returns back to this house, then Saul will answer him. We will not tempt the Thunderer.

ADRIEL: I have it sure, from Eliab his brother, that David was anointed by Samuel to be King over Israel, secretly, in the house of his father Jesse. And Eliab liketh not the youngster, saying he was ever heady, naughty-hearted, full of a youngling's naughty pride, and the conceit of the father's favourite. Now the tale is out in Judah, and many would have him King, saying: Why should Judah look to a King out of Benjamin? Is there no horn-anointed among the men of Judah?

SAUL: So is it! So is it!—To-morrow he shall go forth with his men, and the hand of the Philistine shall be upon him. I will not lift my hand upon him, for fear of the Dark! Yet where is he now? What is he conniving at this moment, in the house of Saul? Go, see what he is about, O Adriel!

[*Exit* ADRIEL.]

ABNER: It is a bad thing, O Saul, to let this jealous worm eat into a King's heart, that always was noble!

SAUL: I cannot help it. The worm is there. And since the women sang—nay, in all the cities they sang the same—*Saul hath slain his thousands, but David hath slain his tens of thousands,* it gnaws me, Abner, and I feel I am no longer King in the sight of the Lord.

ABNER: Canst thou not speak with the Morning Wind? And if the Lord of Days have chosen David to be king over Israel after thee, canst thou not answer the great Wish of the Heavens, saying: *It is well!?*

SAUL: I cannot! I cannot deny my house, and my blood! I cannot cast down my own seed, for the seed of

Scene XI   DAVID   75

Jesse to sprout. I cannot! Wellah, and I will not! Speak not to me of this!

ABNER: Yet wert *thou* chosen of God! And always hast thou been a man of the bright horn.

SAUL: Yea, and am I brought to this pass! Yea, and must I cut myself off? Almost will I rather be a man of Belial, and call on Baal. Surely Astaroth were better to me. For I have kept the faith, yet must I cut myself off! Wellah, is there no other strength?

ABNER: I know not. Thou knowest, who hast heard the thunder and hast felt the Thunderer.

SAUL: I hear It no more, for It hath closed Its lips to me. But other voices hear I in the night—other voices!

[*Enter* ADRIEL.]

SAUL: Well, and where is he?

ADRIEL: He is sitting in the house of Jonathan, and they make music together, so the women listen.

SAUL: Ah! And sings the bird of Bethlehem? What songs now?

ADRIEL: Even to the Lord: *How excellent is thy name in all the earth.* And men and women listen diligently, to learn as it droppeth from his mouth. And Jonathan, for very love, writes it down.

SAUL: Nay, canst thou not remember?

ADRIEL: I cannot, O King. Hark!

[*A man is heard in the courtyard, singing loud and manly, from Psalm viii.*]

Voice of singer: What is man, that thou art mindful of him? and the son of man, that thou visitest him?

For thou hast made him a little lower than the angels, and hast crowned him with glory and honour.

Thou madest him to have dominion over the works
of thy hands;
Thou hast put all things under his feet:
All sheep and oxen, yea, and the beasts of the field;
The fowl of the air, and the fish of the sea, and
whatsoever passeth through the paths of the seas.
O Lord our Lord, how excellent is thy name in all
the earth!

[SAUL *listens moodily*.]

SAUL: I hear him! Yea, they sing after him! He will
set all Israel singing after him, and all men in all
lands. All the world will sing what he sings. And I
shall be dumb. Yea, I shall be dumb, and the lips of
my house will be dust! What, am I naught; and set
at naught! What do I know? Shall I go down into
the grave silenced, and like one mute with ignorance?
Ha! Ha! There are wells in the desert that go deep.
An even there we water the sheep, when our faces
are blackened with drought. Hath Saul no sight into
the unseen? Ha, look! look down the deep well, how
the black water is troubled.—Yea, and I see death,
death, death! I see a sword through my body, and
the body of Jonathan gaping wounds, and my son
Abinadab, and my son Melchishua, and my son Ish-
bosheth lying in blood. Nay, I see the small pale issue of my house creeping on broken feet, as a lamed
worm. Yea, yea, what an end! And the seed of David
rising up and covering the earth, many, with a glory
about them, and the wind of the Lord in their hair.
Nay, then they wheel against the sun, and are dark,
like the locusts sweeping in heaven, like the pillars
of locusts moving, yea, as a tall, dark cloud upon
the land. Till they drop in drops of blood, like

thunder-rain, and the land is red. Then they turn again into the glory of the Lord. Yea, as a flight of birds down all the ages, now shedding sun and the gleam of God, now shedding shadow and the fall of blood, now as quails chirping in the spring, now as the locust pillars of cloud, as death upon the land. And they thicken and thicken, till the world's air grates and clicks as with the wings of locusts. And man is his own devourer, and the Deep turns away, without wish to look on him further. So the earth is a desert, and manless, yet covered with houses and iron. Yea, David, the pits are digged even under the feet of thy God, and thy God shall fall in. Oh, their God shall fall into the pit, that the sons of David have digged. Oh, men can dig a pit for the most high God, and He falls in—as they say of the huge elephant in the lands beyond the desert. And the world shall be Godless, there shall no God walk on the mountains, no whirlwind shall stir like a heart in the deeps of the blue firmament. And God shall be gone from the world. Only men there shall be, in myriads, like locusts, clicking and grating upon one another, and crawling over one another. The smell of them shall be as smoke, but it shall rise up into the air, without finding the nostrils of God. For God shall be gone! gone! gone! And men shall inherit the earth! Yea, like locusts and whirring on wings like locusts. To this the seed of David shall come, and this is their triumph, when the house of Saul has been swept up, long, long ago into the body of God. Godless the world! Godless the men in myriads even like locusts. No God in the air! No God on the mountains! Even out of the deeps of the sky they lured Him, into their pit! So the world is empty of God, empty, empty, like a blown egg-shell bunged with wax and floating meaningless. God shall fall Himself into the pit these men shall dig for Him! Ha! Ha! O David's Almighty, even He knows not the depth of the dark wells in the desert, where men may still water their flocks! Ha! Ha! Lord God of Judah, thou peepest not down the pit where the black water twinkles. Ha-ha! Saul peeps and sees the fate that wells up from below! Ha! Lo! Death and blood, what is this Almighty that sees not the pit digged for Him by the children of men? Ha! Ha! saith Saul. Look in the black mirror! Ha!

ABNER: It is not well, O King.

SAUL: Ha! It is very well! It is very well. Let them lay their trap for his Lord. For his Lord will fall into it. Aha! Aha! Give them length of days. I do not ask it.

ABNER: My lord, the darkness is over your heart.

SAUL: And over my eyes! Ha! And on the swim of the dark are visions. What? Are the demons not under all the works of God, as worms are under the roots of the vine? Look! [*Stares transfixed.*]

ABNER [*to* ADRIEL]: Go quickly and bring Jonathan, and David, for the King is prophesying with the spirit of the under-earth.

[*Exit* ADRIEL.]

SAUL: The room is full of demons! I have known it filled with the breath of Might. The glisten of the dark, old movers that first got the world into shape. They say the god was once as a beetle, but vast and dark. And he rolled the earth into a ball, and laid his seed in it. Then he crept clicking away to hide for ever, while the earth brought forth after him. He went down a deep pit. The gods do not die. They go down a deep pit, and live on at the bottom of oblivion. And when a man staggers, he stumbles and falls backwards down the pit—down the pit, down through oblivion after oblivion, where the gods of the past live on. And they laugh, and eat his soul. And the time will come when even the God of David will fall down the endless pit, till He passes the place where the serpent lies living under oblivion, on to where the Beetle of the Beginning lives under many layers of dark. I see it! Aha! I see the Beetle clambering upon Him, Who was the Lord of Hosts.

ABNER: I cannot hear thee, O King. I would e'en be deaf in this hour. Peace! I bid thee! Peace!

SAUL: What? Did someone speak within the shadow? Come thou forth then from the shadow, if thou hast aught to say.

ABNER: I say Peace! Peace, thou! Say thou no more!

SAUL: What? Peace! saith the voice? And what is peace? Hath the Beetle of the Beginning peace, under many layers of oblivion? Or the great serpent coiled for ever, is he coiled upon his own peace?

[*Enter* JONATHAN, DAVID, *and* MEN.]

SAUL [*continuing*]: I tell you, till the end of time, unrest will come upon the serpent of serpents, and he will lift his head and hiss against the children of men —thus will he hiss! [SAUL *hisses.*] *Hiss! Hiss!* and he will strike the children of men—thus——

[SAUL *strikes as a serpent, and with his javelin.*]

JONATHAN: Father, shall we sound music?

SAUL: Father! Who is father? Know ye not, the vast, dark, shining beetle was the first father, who laid his eggs in a dead ball of the dust of forgotten gods? And out of the egg the serpent of gold, who was great Lord of Life, came forth.

JONATHAN [to DAVID]: Now sing, that peace may come back upon us.

DAVID: If he heed me. [Sings Psalm viii.]

[SAUL meanwhile raves—then sinks into gloom, staring fixedly.]

SAUL: And the serpent was golden with life. But he said to himself: I will lay an egg. So he laid the egg of his own undoing. And the Great White Bird came forth. Some say a dove, some say an eagle, some say a swan, some say a goose—all say a bird. And the serpent of the sun's life turned dark, as all the gods turn dark. Yea, and the Great White Bird beat wings in the firmament, so the dragon slid into a hole, the serpent crawled out of sight, down to the oblivion of oblivion, yet above the oblivion of the Beetle.

[DAVID meanwhile sings.]

SAUL: [striking with his hands as if at a wasp]: Na-a! But what is this sound that comes like a hornet at my ears, and will not let me prophesy! Away! Away!

JONATHAN: My Father, it is a new song to sing.

SAUL: What art thou, Jonathan, thy father's enemy?

JONATHAN: Listen to the new song, Father.

SAUL: What? [Hearkens a moment.] I will not hear it! What! I say I will not hear it! Trouble me not, nor stop the dark fountain of my prophecy! I will not hearken! [Listens.]

DAVID [singing]: When I consider thy heavens, the work of thy fingers, the moon and the stars, which thou hast ordained.

SAUL: What! art thou there, thou brown hornet, thou

stealer of life's honey! What, shalt thou stay in my sight! [*Suddenly hurls his javelin at* DAVID. DAVID *leaps aside.*]

JONATHAN: My Father, this shall not be!

SAUL: What! art thou there? Bring me here my dart.

JONATHAN [*picking up the javelin*]: Look then at the hole in the wall! Is not that a reproach against the house of the King for ever? [*Gives the javelin to* SAUL.]

[SAUL *sinks into moody silence, staring.* DAVID *begins to sing very softly.*]

DAVID [*singing*]: O Lord our Lord, how excellent is thy name in all the earth! Who hast set thy glory above the heavens.

[SAUL *very softly, with the soft, swift suddenness of a great cat, leaps round and hurls the javelin again.* DAVID *as swiftly leaps aside.*]

SAUL: I will smite David even to the wall.

ABNER: Go hence, David! Swiftly hence!

JONATHAN: Twice, Father!

[*Exit* DAVID.]

ABNER [*seizing javelin*]: The evil spirits upon thee have done this. O Saul! They have not prevailed.

SAUL: Have I pierced him? Is he down with the dead? Can we lay him in the sides of the pit?

ABNER: He is not dead! He is gone forth.

SAUL [*wearily*]: Gone forth! Ay! He is gone forth!— What, did I seek to slay him?

JONATHAN: Yea, twice.

SAUL: It was out of myself. I was then beside myself.

ABNER: Yea, the evil spirits were upon thee.

SAUL: Tell him, O Jonathan, Saul seeks not his life. Nay! Nay! Do I not love him, even as thou dost, but more, even as a father! O David! David! I have loved thee. Oh, I have loved thee and the Lord in thee.—And now the evil days have come upon me, and I have thrown the dart against thee, and against the Lord. I am a man given over to trouble, and tossed between two winds. Lo, how can I walk before the faces of men! [*Covers his face with his mantle.*]

ABNER: The evil spirits have left him. Peace comes with sorrow.

JONATHAN: And only then.

SAUL: Bring David hither to me, for I will make my peace with him, for my heart is very sore.

JONATHAN: Verily, shall it be peace?

SAUL: Yea! For I fear the Night. [*Exit* JONATHAN.] Surely now will David publish it in Judah: *Saul hath lifted his hand to slay me.*

ABNER: He will not publish it in Judah.

SAUL: And wherefore not? Is he not as the apple of their eyes to the men of Judah, who love not overmuch the tribe of Benjamin?

ABNER: But David is the King's man.

SAUL: Ah, would it were verily so.

[*Enter* JONATHAN *and* DAVID.]

DAVID: The Lord strengthen the King!

SAUL: Ah, David, my son, come, and come in peace. For my hands are bare and my heart is washed and my eyes are no longer deluded. May the Lord be with thee, David, and hold it not against me, what I have done. Spirits of the earth possess me, and I am not my own. Thou shalt not cherish it in thy heart, what Saul did against thee, in the season of his bewilderment?

DAVID: Naught has the King done against me. And the heart of thy servant knoweth no ill.

SAUL: Hatest thou me not, David?

DAVID: Let the word be unspoken, my Father!

SAUL: Ah, David! David! Why can I not love thee untroubled?—But I will right the wrong.—Thou shalt henceforth be captain of the thousand of Hebron, and dwell in thine own house, by the men. And behold, Merab, my elder daughter, I will give thee to wife.

DAVID: Who am I, and what is my life, or my father's family in Israel, that I should be son-in-law to the King?

SAUL: Nay, thou art of mine own heart, and the Lord is thy great strength. Only be valiant for me, and fight the Lord's battles.

DAVID: All my life is the King's, and my strength is to serve.

SAUL: It shall be well. And with thy thousand shalt thou succour Israel.

CURTAIN

SCENE XII

The well at Gilgal: MAIDENS *coming with water-jars. Two* HERDSMEN *filling the trough—one below, at the water, one on the steps. They swing the leathern bucket back and forth with a rough chant: the lower shepherd swinging the load to the upper, who swings it to the trough, and hands it back.* DAVID *approaching.*

1ST HERDSMAN: Ya! David missed her.
2ND HERDSMAN: Let him get her sister—Oh! Oh-oh-h!
1ST HERDSMAN: Ya! David missed her.
2ND HERDSMAN: Let him get her sister—Oh-h-h-h!
   [*Continue several times.*]
1ST MAIDEN: How long, O Herdsman!
2ND HERDSMAN: Ho-o-o! Enough!
1ST HERDSMAN [*coming up*]: Ya! David missed her!
   [MAIDENS *run away from him.*]
1ST MAIDEN: Ho, thou! Seest thou not David?
1ST HERDSMAN: Yea, he is there! Ho! David! And hast thou missed her?
DAVID: What sayest thou, O Man?
1ST HERDSMAN: Thou hast missed her—say!—am I not right?
DAVID: And whom have I missed?
1ST HERDSMAN: Wellah! And knowest thou not?
DAVID: Nay!

1ST HERDSMAN: Wellah! But Merab, the King's elder daughter! Wellah! We feasted her week half a moon ago, whilst you and your men were gone forth against the Philistines. Wellah, man, and didst thou not know?

DAVID: Sayest thou so?

1ST HERDSMAN: Wellah! And is it not so? Say, Maidens, hath not Adriel the Meholathite got Merab, Saul's daughter, to wife? And hath he not spent his week with her? Wellah, thou art ousted from that bed, O David.

DAVID: And hath the King given his daughter Merab unto Adriel the Meholathite! Wellah, shall he not do as he choose, with his own?

1ST HERDSMAN: Ay, wellah, shall he! But thou wert promised. And in thy stead, another hath gone in unto her. Is it not so, O Maidens? Sleeps not Merab in the tent of Adriel the Meholathite?

1ST MAIDEN: Yea, the King hath married her to the man.

DAVID: And sings she as she shakes his butter-skin?

1ST MAIDEN: Nay, as yet she sings not. But if David sits here beneath the tree, she will come with her jar. Nay, is that not Adriel the Meholathite himself, coming forth? O Herdsman, drive not the cattle as yet to the drinking troughs!

[*Goes down and fills her pitcher.*]

2ND MAIDEN: Will David sit awhile beneath the tree?

DAVID: Yea!

2ND MAIDEN: Then shall Michal, daughter of Saul, come hither with her water-jar. Is it well, O David?

DAVID: Yea, it is very well.

[MAIDEN *goes down with her pitcher.*]

ADRIEL: Ha, David! And art thou returned? I have not seen thee before the King.

DAVID: I returned but yesterday. And I saw the King at the dawn. Now art thou become a great man in Israel, O Adriel, and son-in-law to the King. How fareth Merab in the tents of the Meholathite?

ADRIEL: Yea, and blithely. And to-morrow even in the early day will I set her on an ass, and we will get us to my father's house. For he is old, and the charge of his possessions is heavy upon him, and he fain would see his daughter Merab, who shall bring him sons—sons to gladden him. And she shall have her hand-maidens about her, and her store-barns of wool, and corn, and clotted figs, and bunches of raisins, all her wealth she shall see in store!

DAVID: May she live content, and bring thee sons, even males of worth.

ADRIEL: The Lord grant it! And thou hast come home once more with spoil! How thou chastenest the Philistine! Yea, and behold, the King hath delight in thee, and all his servants love thee! Lo! I am the King's son-in-law, of Merab. Now, therefore, be thou also the King's son-in-law, for there is yet a daughter.

DAVID: Seemeth it to you a light thing, to be the King's son-in-law, seeing that I am a poor man, and lightly esteemed?

ADRIEL: By my beard, the King delighteth in thee, and all his servants love thee. There is no man in Israel more fit to take a daughter of the King.

DAVID: Yea, there be men of mighty substance such as thou, whose flocks have not been counted, and who send men-at-arms pricking with iron lance-points, to the King's service. But what have I, save the bare hands and heart of a faithful servant?

ADRIEL: Nay, thy name is high among men. But lo! here cometh Saul, as he hath promised. He is coming out to my tents. I will go forward to bring him in. Come thou?

DAVID: Nay! Leave me here.
[*Exit* ADRIEL.]

1ST HERDSMAN: I have heard the mouth of Adriel, O David! Surely he is the King's listener.

DAVID: And thou! Who made *thee* a listener?

1ST HERDSMAN: Nay, I must guard the water-troughs till the cattle have drunk. Adriel hath flocks and men-servants, but David hath the Lord, and the hearts of all Israel! Better a brave and bright man, with a face that shines to the heart, than a great owner of troops and herds, who struts with arms akimbo. As I plant this driving-stick in the soft earth, so hath the Lord planted David in the heart of Israel. I say: Stick, may thou flourish! May thou bud and blossom and be a great tree. For thou art not as the javelin of Saul, levelled at David's bosom.

DAVID: Peace! Saul cometh.

1ST HERDSMAN: Wellah! And I will go down to the water.
[*Goes to the well.*]

DAVID: The Lord strengthen the King.

SAUL: Art thou my son, David? Yea, David, have they told thee, I have married my daughter Merab unto Adriel the Meholathite, even to him who stands here?

DAVID: Yea, O Saul! They told me the King's pleasure. May the Lord bless thy house for ever!

SAUL: Have I not promised my daughter unto thee? But my servants tell me the heart of Michal goes forth wishful unto David. Say now, is she fair in thine eyes?

DAVID: Yea! Yea, O King, yea!

SAUL: When the new moon shows her tender horns above the west, thou shalt this day be my son-in-law in one of the twain.

DAVID: Let thy servant but serve the King!

SAUL: Yea, an thou serve me, it shall be on the day of the new moon.

DAVID: Yea, will I serve without fail.

SAUL: So be it!

[*Exit with* ADRIEL.]

HERDSMAN [*coming up*]: Now is David the richest man in Israel—in promises! Wilt thou not sell me a King's promise, for this my camel-stick?

DAVID: It is well.

HERDSMAN: Sayest thou? Then it is a bargain? Wellah! Take my stick. It is worth the word of a King.

DAVID: Peace!

HERDSMAN: Thou meanest *war!*

DAVID: How?

HERDSMAN: If thou get her, it is war. If thou get her not, it is more war. Sayest thou peace?

MAIDENS [*running*]: Oh, master David, hath Saul passed with Adriel?

HERDSMAN: They have passed, letting fall promises as the goat droppeth pills.

DAVID: Peace, O Man!

MAIDEN: Oh, master David, shall Michal come forth to fill her water-jar? For Merab is setting meats before the King, in the booth of Adriel. Oh, David, shall Michal bring her jar to the well?

HERDSMAN: Ay, wellah, shall she! And I will hold back the cattle this little while, for I hear their voices.
 [*Exit.*]

DAVID: Run back quickly and let her come.
 [*Exit* MAIDEN.]

DAVID [*alone*]: Lord! dost Thou send this maiden to me? My entrails strain in me, for Michal, daughter of Saul. Lord God of my Salvation, my wanting of this maiden is next to my wanting Thee. My body is a strong-strung bow. Lord, let me shoot mine arrow unto this mark. Thou fillest me with desire as with thunder, Thy lightning is in my loins, and my breast like a cloud leans forward for her. Lord! Lord! Thy left hand is about her middle, and Thy right hand grasps my life. So Thou bringest us together in Thy secret self, that it may be fulfilled for Thee in us. Lord of the Great Wish, I will not let her go.

MICHAL [*entering—covering her chin and throat with her kerchief*]: Wilt thou let me pass to fill my jar, O thou stranger?

DAVID: Come, Michal, and I will fill thy jar.
 [*She comes forward—he takes her jar and goes down the steps. Returning he sets it on the ground at his feet.*]

MICHAL: Oh, David! And art thou still unslain?

DAVID: As the Lord wills, no man shall slay me. And livest thou in thine house lonely, without thy sister Merab?

MICHAL: Is thy heart sore in thee, David, that thou

hast lost Merab? Her heart is gentle, and she sighed for thee. But e'en she obeyed.

DAVID: She hath a man of more substance than David. And my heart is very glad on her account.

MICHAL: It is well.

DAVID: O Michal, didst thou come willingly to the well, when the maiden told thee I waited here?

MICHAL: Yea, willingly.

DAVID: O Michal, my heart runs before me, when it sees thee far off, like one eager to come to his own place. Oh, thou with the great eyes of the wilderness, shall my heart leap to thee, and shall thou not say Nay! to it?

MICHAL: What said my father, O David, when he passed?

DAVID: He said: when the new moon showeth her horns in the west, on this day shalt thou surely be my son-in-law of one of the twain.

MICHAL: Yea, and is thy heart uplifted, to be a King's son-in-law?

DAVID: So she be Michal, my body is uplifted like the sail of a ship when the wind arouses.

MICHAL: Nay, thou art a seeker of honours! Merab had been just as well to thy liking.

DAVID: Ah, no! Ah! Ah! Merab is gentle and good, and my heart softened with kindness for her, as a man unto a woman. But thou art like the rising moon, that maketh the limbs of the mountain glisten. O Michal, we twain are upon the hillsides of the Lord, and surely He will bring our strength together!

MICHAL: And if the Lord God say thee nay!

DAVID: He will not. He hath thy life in His left hand, and my life He holdeth in His right hand. And surely He will lay us together in the secret of His desire, and I shall come unto thee by the Lord's doing.

MICHAL: But if He say thee nay, thou wilt let me go.

DAVID: Thou knowest not the Lord my God. The flame He kindles He will not blow out. He is not yea-and-nay! But my Lord my God loveth a bright desire and yearneth over a great Wish, for its fulfilment. Oh, the Lord my God is a glowing flame and He loveth all things that do glow. So loves He thee, Michal, O woman before me, for thou glowest like a young tree in full flower, with flowers of gold and scarlet, and dark leaves. O thou young pomegranate tree, flowers and fruit together show on thy body. And flame calleth to flame, for flame is the body of God, like flowers of flame. Oh, and God is a great Wish, and a great Desire, and a pure flame for ever. Thou art kindled of the Lord, O Michal, and He will not let thee go.

MICHAL: Yet the Lord Himself will not marry me.

DAVID: I will marry thee, for the Lord hath kindled me unto thee, and hath said: Go to her, for the fruits of the pomegranate are ripe.

MICHAL: Will thou not seek me for thyself?

DAVID: Yea, for my very self; and for my very self; and for the Lord's own self in me.

MICHAL: Ever thou puttest the Lord between me and thee.

DAVID: The Lord is a sweet wind that fills thy bosom and thy belly as the sail of a ship; so I see thee sailing delicately towards me, borne onwards by my Lord.

MICHAL: Oh, David, would the new moon were come! For I fear my father, and I misdoubt his hindrances.

DAVID: Thinkest thou, he would marry thee away, as Merab?

MICHAL: Nay, but thou must make a song, and sing it before all Israel, that Michal is thine by the King's promise, no man shall look on her but David.

DAVID: Yea! I will make a song. And yea, I will not let thee go. Thou shalt come to me as wife, and I will know thee, and thou shall lie in my bosom. Yea! As the Lord liveth!

MICHAL: And as the Lord liveth, not even my father shall constrain me, to give me to another man, before the new moon showeth her horns.

DAVID: It is well, O Michal! O Michal, wife of David, thou shalt sleep in my tent! In the tent of the men of war, beside the sword of David, Michal sleeps, and the hand of David is upon her hip. He has sealed her with his seal, and Michal of David is her name, and kingdoms shall he bring down to her. Michal of David shall blossom in the land, her name shall blossom in the mouths of soldiers as the rose of Sharon after rain. And men-at-arms shall shout her name, like a victory cry it shall be heard. And she shall be known in the land but as Michal of David; blossom of God, keeper of David's nakedness.

MICHAL: They shall not reive me from thee.—I see men coming.

DAVID: Wilt thou go?

MICHAL: I shall call my maidens. So ho! So ho! [*Waves the end of her kerchief.*]

HERDSMAN [*entering*]: There are two captains, servants

of Saul coming even now from the booths of the Meholathite, where the King is.

MICHAL: Yea, let them come, and we will hear the words they put forth.

HERDSMAN: And the cattle are being driven round by the apricot garden. They will soon be here.

DAVID: In two words we shall have the mind of Saul from these captains.

MAIDENS [*entering—running*]: O Michal, men are approaching!

MICHAL: Fill you your jar, and with one ear let us listen. David stays under the tree.

1ST MAIDEN: Stars are in thine eyes, O Michal, like a love night!

2ND MAIDEN: Oh! and the perfume of a new-opened flower! What sweetness has she heard?

3RD MAIDEN: Oh, say! what words like honey, and like new sweet dates of the Oasis, hath David the singer said to Michal? Oh, that we might have heard!

1ST CAPTAIN [*entering*]: David is still at the well?

DAVID: Yea, after war and foray, happy is the homely passage at the well?

2ND CAPTAIN: Wilt thou return to the King's house with us, and we will tell thee what is toward: even the words of Saul concerning thee.

DAVID: Say on! For I must in the other way.

1ST CAPTAIN: The King delighteth in thee more than in any man of Israel. For no man layeth low the King's enemies like David, in the land.

DAVID: Sayest thou so?

1ST CAPTAIN: Yea! And when the new moon shows her horns shalt thou be son-in-law to Saul, in his daughter Michal.

DAVID: As the Lord, and the King, willeth. Saul hath said as much to me, even now. Yet I am a poor man, and how shall the King at last accept me?

2ND CAPTAIN: This too hath Saul considered. And he hath said: Tell my son David, the King desireth not any bride-money, nay, neither sheep nor oxen nor asses, nor any substance of his. But an hundred foreskins of the Philistines shall he bring to the King, to be avenged of his enemies.

1ST CAPTAIN: So said the King: Before the new moon, as she cometh, sets on her first night, shall David bring the foreskins of an hundred Philistines unto Saul. And that night shall Saul deliver Michal, his daughter, unto David, and she shall sleep in David's house.

2ND CAPTAIN: And Israel shall be avenged of her enemies.

DAVID: Hath the King verily sent this message to me?

1ST CAPTAIN: Yea, he hath sent it, and a ring from his own hand. Lo! here it is! For said Saul: Let David keep this for a pledge between me and him, in this matter. And when he returneth, he shall give me my ring again, and the foreskins of the Philistine, and I will give him my daughter Michal to wife.

DAVID: Yea! Then I must hence, and call my men, and go forth against the Philistine. For while the nights yet are moonless, and without point of moon, will I return with the tally.

[*Exit.*]

2ND CAPTAIN: Yea, he is gone on the King's errand.

1ST CAPTAIN: Let him meet what the King wishes.

[*Exeunt.*]

HERDSMAN: Yea, I know what ye would have. Ye would

slay David with the sword of the Philistine. For who keeps promise with a dead man! [MICHAL *and* MAIDENS *edge in.*] Hast thou heard, O Michal? David is gone forth against the Philistine. For Saul asketh an hundred foreskins of the enemy as thy bride-money. Is it not a tall dowry?

MICHAL: Yea! hath my father done this!

HERDSMAN: Wellah, hath he! For dead men marry no kings' daughters. And the spear of some Philistine shall beget death in the body of David. Thy father hath made thee dear!

MICHAL: Nay, he hath made my name cheap in all Israel.

2ND HERDSMAN [*entering*]: Run, Maidens! The cattle are coming round the wall, athirst!

MAIDENS [*shouldering their jars*]: Away! Away!
 [*Exeunt.*]

CURTAIN

SCENE XIII

A room in DAVID's *house in Gilgal. Almost dark.* DAVID *alone, speaking softly: an image in a corner.*

DAVID: Give ear to my words, O Lord, consider my meditation.
Hearken unto the voice of my cry, my King, and my God: for unto thee will I pray.
My voice shalt thou hear in the morning, O Lord; in the morning will I direct my prayer unto thee, and will look up.
For thou art not a God that hath pleasure in wickedness: neither shall evil dwell with thee.
The foolish shall not stand in thy sight: thou hatest all workers of iniquity.
Thou shalt destroy them that speak leasing: the Lord will abhor the bloody and deceitful man.
But as for me, I will come into thy house in the multitude of thy mercy: and in thy fear will I worship toward thy holy temple.
Lead me, O Lord, in thy righteousness, because of mine enemies; make thy way straight before my face.
For there is no faithfulness in their mouth; their inward part is very wickedness; their throat is an open sepulchre: they flatter with their tongue.
Destroy thou them, O God; let them fall by their

Scene XIII   DAVID

own counsel; cast them out in the multitude of
their transgressions; for they have rebelled
against thee.
But let all those that put their trust in thee rejoice:
let them ever shout for joy, because thou de-
fendest them: let them also that love thy name
be joyful in thee.
For thou, Lord, wilt bless the righteous; with favour
wilt thou compass him, as with a shield.

Pause

Nay, Lord, I am Thy anointed, and Thy son. With the
oil of anointment hast Thou begotten me. Oh, I am
twice begotten: of Jesse, and of God! I go forth as a
son of God, and the Lord is with me. Yet for this
they hate me, and Saul seeks to destroy me. What
can I do, O Lord, in this pass?
   [*Enter* MICHAL, *through curtain at side, with
   tray and lamp.*]
MICHAL: The dawn is at hand. Art thou not faint with
this long watching before the Lord? Oh! why wilt
thou leave thy bed and thy pleasure of the night, to
speak out into the empty, chill hour towards morning? Come then, eat of the food which I have
brought.
DAVID: I will not eat now, for my soul still yearns away
from me.
MICHAL: Art thou sick?
DAVID: Yea! My soul is sick.
MICHAL: Why?
DAVID: Nay, thou knowest. Thy father hates me beyond measure.

MICHAL: But I love you.

DAVID [*takes her hand*]: Yea!

MICHAL: Is it nothing to you that Michal is your wife and loves you?

DAVID: Verily, it is not nothing. But, Michal, what will come to me at last? From moon to moon Saul's anger waxes. I shall lose my life at last. And what good shall I be to thee then?

MICHAL: Ah, no! Ah, no! Never shall I see thee dead. First thou shalt see me dead. Never, never shall I tear my hair for thee, as a widow. It shall not be. If thou go hence, it shall not be into death.

DAVID: Yet death is near. From month to month, since I came back with the foreskins of the Philistine, and got thee to wife, Saul has hated me more. Michal loves David, and Saul's hate waxes greater. Jonathan loves David, and the King commands Jonathan, saying: There, where thou seest him, there shalt thou slay David.

MICHAL: My father is no more a man. He is given over entirely to evil spirits. But Jonathan will save thee through it all.

DAVID: The Lord will save me. And Jonathan is dearer to me than a heart's brother.

MICHAL: Think, O husband, if Saul hateth thee, how Michal and Jonathan, who are children of Saul, do love thee.

DAVID: Yea, verily! It is like the rainbow in the sky unto me. But, O Michal, how shall we win through? I have loved Saul. And I have not it in me to hate him. Only his perpetual anger puts on me a surpassing heaviness, and a weariness, so my flesh wearies upon my bones.

Scene XIII DAVID 99

MICHAL: But why? Why? Why does it matter to thee? I love thee, all the time.—Jonathan loves thee.—Thy men love thee. Why does the frenzy of one distracted man so trouble thee? Why? It is out of all measure.

DAVID: Nay, he is Saul, and the Lord's anointed. And he is King over all Israel.

MICHAL: And what then? He is no man among men any more. Evil possesses him. Why heed him, and wake in the night for him?

DAVID: Because he is the Lord's anointed, and one day he will kill me.

MICHAL: He will never kill thee. Thou sayest thyself, the Lord will prevent him. And if not the Lord, then I will prevent him—for I am not yet nothing in Gilgal. And Jonathan will prevent him. And the captains will prevent him. And art thou not also the Lord's anointed? And will not the Lord set thee King on the hill of Zion, in thine own Judah?

DAVID: O Michal! O Michal! That the hand of the Lord's anointed should be lifted against the Lord's anointed! What can I do? For Saul is the Lord's, and I may not even see an enemy in him. I cannot, verily! Yet he seeks to slay me. All these months since he gave thee to me, after I brought the foreskins of the Philistine for thy dowry, he has hated me more, and sought my life. Before the moon of our marriage was waned away thy father commanded his servants, and even Jonathan, to slay David on that spot where they should find him. So Jonathan came to me in haste and secret, and sent me away into the fields by night and hid me. Yea, before the month of our marriage was finished I had to flee from thee in the night, and leave my place cold.

MICHAL: But not for long. Not for long. Jonathan persuaded my father, so he took thee back. Even he loved thee again.

DAVID: Yea, he also loves me! But Saul is a man falling backward down a deep pit, that must e'en clutch what is nearest him, and drag it down along with him.

MICHAL: But Saul swore: As the Lord liveth, David shall not be slain.

DAVID: Ay, he swore. But before two moons were passed his brow was black again. And when the season of the year came, that the Kings of the Philistine go forth, I went up against them, and fought. The months of the fighting I fought with them, and all the people rejoiced. But I saw with a sinking heart the face of Saul blacken, blacken darker with greater hate! Yea, he hath loved me, as the Lord's anointed must love the Lord's anointed. But Saul is slipping backward down the pit of despair, away from God. And each time he strives to come forth, the loose earth yields beneath his feet, and he slides deeper. So the upreach of his love fails him, and the downslide of his hate is great and greater in weight. I cannot hate him—nor love him—but, O Michal, I am oppressed with a horror of him.

MICHAL: Nay, do not dwell on him.

DAVID: And the year went round its course, and once more there was war with the Philistine. And once more we prevailed, in the Lord. And once more the armies shouted my name. And once more I came home to thee—and thou didst sing. And my heart did sing above thee. But as a bird hushes when the shadow of the hawk dances upon him from heaven, my heart went hushed under the shadow of Saul. And my heart could not sing between thy breasts, as it wanted to, even the heart of a bridegroom. For the shadow of Saul was upon it.

MICHAL: Oh, why do you care? Why do you care? Why do you not love me and never care?

DAVID: It is not in me. I have been blithe of thy love and thy body. But now three days ago, even in the midst of my blitheness, Saul again threw his javelin at me—yea, even in the feast. And I am marked among all men. And the end draws nigh.—For scarce may I leave this house, lest at some corner they slay me.

MICHAL: What end, then? What end draws nigh?

DAVID: I must get me gone. I must go into the wilderness.

MICHAL [*weeping*]: Oh, bitter! Bitter! My joy has been torn from me, as an eagle tears a lamb from the ewe. I have no joy in my life, nor in the body of my lord and my husband. A serpent is hid in my marriage bed, my joy is venomed. Oh, that they had wed me to a man that moved me not, rather than be moved to so much hurt.

DAVID: Nay, nay! Oh, nay, nay! Between me and thee is no bitterness, and between my body and thy body there is constant joy! Nay, nay! Thou art a flame to me of man's forgetting, and God's presence. Nay, nay! Thou shalt not weep for me, for thou art a delight to me, even a delight and a forgetting.

MICHAL: No! No! Thou leavest me in the night, to make prayers and moaning before the Lord. Oh, that thou hadst never married in thy body the daughter of thine enemy!

DAVID: Say not so, it is a wrong thing; thou art sweet to me, and all my desire.

MICHAL: It is not true! Thou moanest, and leavest me in the night, to fall before the Lord.

DAVID: Yea, trouble is come upon me. And I must take my trouble to the Lord. But thy breasts are my bliss and my forgetting. Oh, do not remember my complaining! But let thyself be sweet to me, and let me sleep among the lilies.

MICHAL: Thou wilt reproach me again with my father.

DAVID: Ah, no! Ah, never I reproached thee! But now I can forget, I can forget all but thee, and the blossom of thy sweetness. Oh, come with me, and let me know thee. For thou art ever again as new to me.

MICHAL [*rising as he takes her hand*]: Nay, thou wilt turn the bitterness of thy spirit upon me again.

DAVID: Ah, no! I will not! But the gate of my life can I open to thee again, and the world of bitterness shall be gone under as in a flood.

MICHAL: And wilt thou not leave me?

DAVID: Nay, lift up thy voice no more, for the hour of speech has passed.

[*Exeunt through curtain at back.*]

SCENE XIV

The same room, unchanged, an hour or so later: but the grey light of day. A WOMAN-SERVANT *comes in. There is a wooden image in a corner.*

WOMAN-SERVANT: Yea, the lighted lamp, and the food! My lord David hath kept watch again before the Lord, and tears will fall on Michal's bosom, and darken her heart! Aiee! Aiee! That Saul should so hate the life of David! Surely the evil spirits are strong upon the King.
BOY [*entering*]: Jonathan, the King's son, is below, knocking softly at the door.
WOMAN-SERVANT: Go! Open swiftly, and make fast again. Aiee! Aiee! My lord Jonathan comes too early for a pleasure visit. I will see if they sleep. [*Goes through the curtain.*]
    [*Enter* JONATHAN. JONATHAN *stands silent, pensive. Goes to window. Re-enter* WOMAN-SERVANT. *She starts, seeing* JONATHAN—*then puts her hand on her mouth.*]
WOMAN-SERVANT: O my lord Jonathan! Hush!
JONATHAN: They are sleeping still?
WOMAN-SERVANT: They are sleeping the marriage sleep. David hath even watched before the Lord, in the night. But now with Michal he sleeps the marriage sleep, in the lands of peace. Now grant a son shall

come of it, to ease the gnawing of Michal's heart.

JONATHAN: What gnaws in Michal's heart?

WOMAN-SERVANT: Ah, my lord, her love even for David, that will not be appeased. If the Giver gave her a son, so should her love for David abate, and cease to gnaw in her.

JONATHAN: But why should it gnaw in her? Hath she not got him, and the joy of him?

WOMAN-SERVANT: O Jonathan, she is even as the house of Saul. What she hath cannot appease her.

JONATHAN: What then would she more?

WOMAN-SERVANT: She is of the house of Saul, and her very love is pain to her. Each cloud that crosses her is another death of her love. Ah, it is better to let love come and to let it go, even as the winds of the hills blow along the heavens. The sun shines, and is dulled, and shines again; it is the day, and its alterings; and after, it is night.

JONATHAN: David and Michal are asleep?

WOMAN-SERVANT: In the marriage sleep. Oh, break it not!

JONATHAN: The sun will soon rise. Lo! this house is upon the wall of the city, and the fields and the hills lie open.

WOMAN-SERVANT: Shall I bring food to Jonathan?

JONATHAN: Nay! Hark! Men are crying at the city's western gate, to open. The day is beginning.

WOMAN-SERVANT: May it bring good to this house!

JONATHAN: It is like to bring evil.

WOMAN-SERVANT: Ah, my lord!

DAVID [*appearing through the curtain at the back*]: Jonathan!

JONATHAN: David! Thou art awake!

DAVID [*laughing*]: Yea! Am I not? Thou art my brother Jonathan, art thou not? [*They embrace.*]

JONATHAN: O David, the darkness was upon my father in the night, and he hath again bid slay thee. Leave not the house. Unbar not the door! Watch! And be ready to flee! If armed men stand round the door [MICHAL *appears*], then let down the boy from the window, and send instantly to me. I will come with thy men and with mine, and we will withstand the hosts of Saul, if need be.

MICHAL: Is something new toward?

JONATHAN: My father bade his men take David, and slay him in the dawn. I must away, lest they see that I have warned thee. Farewell, O David!

DAVID: Farewell, my brother Jonathan! But I will come down the stair with thee.

[*Exeunt.*]

MICHAL: Yea! Yea! So sure as it is well between me and him, so sure as we have peace in one another, so sure as we are together—comes this evil wind, and blows upon us! And oh, I am weary of my life, because of it!

WOMAN-SERVANT: Aiee! Aiee! Say not so, O Michal! For thy days are many before thee.

MICHAL: This time, an they take him, they will surely kill him.

WOMAN-SERVANT: Sayest thou so! Oh, why, in the Lord's name!

MICHAL: I know it. If they take him this time, he is lost.

WOMAN-SERVANT: Oh, then shall they surely not take him! Oh, but what shall we do?

MICHAL: Creep thou on the roof! Let no man see thee.

And there lie: watch if armed men approach the house.

DAVID [*entering*]: There is no one there.

MICHAL: They will come as the sun comes. [*To* WOMAN.] Go thou and watch.

WOMAN-SERVANT: Verily I will!
[*Exit.*]

MICHAL: O David! So sure as it is springtime in me, and my body blossoms like an almond-tree, comes this evil wind upon me, and withers my bud! Oh, how can I bring forth children to thee, when the spear of this vexation each time pierces my womb?

DAVID: Trouble not thyself, my flower. No wind shall wither thee.

MICHAL: Oh, but I know. This time, an they take thee, thou shalt lose thy life.—And Jonathan will not save thee.

DAVID: Nay! Be not afraid for me.

MICHAL: Yes! I am afraid! I am afraid! Ho! Ho, there! [*Claps her hands. Enter* BOY. *To* BOY.] Bring the water-skin for thy master, filled with water. And his pouch with bread—for he goeth on a journey.—O David! David! Now take thy cloak, and thy bow, and thy spear, and put on thy shoes. For thou must go! Jonathan cannot avail thee this time.

DAVID: Nay! Why shall I flee, when the sun is rising?

MICHAL: Yea! If thou go not before the sun is here, in the morning shalt thou be slain. Oh, make ready! Thy shoes! Put them on! [DAVID *reluctantly obeys.*] Thy cloak, so they shall not know thee! [*He puts it on.*] Thy spear and bow!

BOY [*entering*]: Here is the pouch and the water-flask.
MICHAL: Run, bring figs and dry curds. Dost thou hear aught at the door?
BOY: Naught!
　　[*Exit.*]
MICHAL: O David, art thou ready! Oh, that thou leavest me!
DAVID: I need not go! Yea, to comfort thee, I will go to the place that Jonathan knoweth of, and thou shalt send thither for me. Or wilt thou——
WOMAN-SERVANT [*re-entering*]: O Michal! O David, master! There be men-at-arms approaching, under the wall, and walking by stealth. Oh, flee! Oh, flee! for they mean thy life.
MICHAL: Now must thou go by the window, into the fields. I see the sun's first glitter. Even for this hour have I kept the new rope ready. [*She fastens the rope to a stout stake, and flings the ends from the window. To* DAVID.] Go! Go! Swiftly be gone!
DAVID: I will come again to thee. Sooner or later, as the Lord liveth, I will take thee again to me, unto my bed and my body.
MICHAL: Hark! They knock! Ha—a!
BOY [*entering*]: There are men at the door!
MICHAL: Go! Call to them! Ask what they want! But touch thou not the door!
　　[DAVID *meanwhile climbs through the window—the stake holds the rope.*]
WOMAN-SERVANT [*climbing with her hands*]: So! So! So! My lord David! So! So! Swing him not against the wall, O spiteful rope. So! So! He kicks free!

Yea! And God be praised, he is on the ground, looking an instant at his hands. So he looks up and departs! Lifts his hand and departs!

MICHAL: Is he gone? Draw in the rope, and hide it safe.

WOMAN-SERVANT: That I will!

> [*Meanwhile* MICHAL *has flung back the curtain of the recess where the low earthen bank of the bed is seen, with skins and covers. She takes the wooden image of a god and lays it in the bed, puts a pillow at its head, and draws the bed-cover high over it.*]

MICHAL [*to herself*]: Yea, and my house's god which is in my house, shall lie in my husband's place, and the image of my family god, which came of old from my mother's house, shall deceive them. For my house has its own gods, yea, from of old [*enter* BOY], and shall they forsake me?

BOY: They demand to enter. The King asketh for David, that he go before the King's presence.

MICHAL: Go thou, say to them: My lord and my master, David, is sick in his bed.

BOY: I will say that.

> [*Exit.*]

WOMAN-SERVANT: Sit thou nigh the bed. And if they still will come up, thou shalt say he sleepeth.

MICHAL: Yea, will I. [*Sits by bed.*] O god of my household, O god of my mother's house, O god in the bed of David, save me now!

> [*Enter* BOY.]

BOY: They will e'en set eyes on my master.

MICHAL: Stay! Say to them, that their captains shall come up, two only: but softly, for my lord David

hath been sick these three days, and at last sleepeth.
BOY: I will tell them.
  [*Exit.*]
WOMAN-SERVANT: And I too will go bid them hush.
  [*Exit.* MICHAL *sits in silence.*]
  [*Enter two* CAPTAINS *with the* WOMAN-SERVANT.]
WOMAN-SERVANT: There he sleepeth in the bed.
MICHAL: Sh-h-h!
1ST CAPTAIN: I will go even now and tell the King.
  [*Exeunt the* CAPTAINS *after a pause.*]

CURTAIN

  [*Curtain rises after a short time on same scene.*]
WOMAN-SERVANT [*rushing in*]: They are coming again down the street, but boldly now.
MICHAL: Yea! Let them come! By this time is David beyond their reach, in the secret place.
WOMAN-SERVANT: Oh, and what shall befall thee! Oh!
MICHAL: I am the King's daughter. Even Saul shall not lift his hand against me. Go down thou to the door, and hold the men whilst thou mayst. Why should we admit them forthwith? Say that Michal is performing her ablutions.
WOMAN-SERVANT: Will I not!
  [*Exit.*]
MICHAL: And shall I strip the bed? They will search the house and the fields. Nay, I will leave it, and they shall see how they were fools. O teraphim, O my god of my own house, hinder them and help me. O thou my teraphim, watch for me!
  [*Sound of knocking below.*]

VOICE OF SERVANT: Ho, ye! Who knocks, in the Lord's name?
VOICE OF CAPTAIN: Open! Open ye! In the name of the King.
VOICE OF SERVANT: What would ye in this house of sickness?
VOICE OF CAPTAIN: Open, and thou shalt know.
VOICE OF SERVANT: I may not open, save Michal bid me.
VOICE OF CAPTAIN: Then bid Michal bid thee open forthwith.
VOICE OF SERVANT: O thou captain of the loud shout, surely thou wert here before! Know then, my master is sick, and my mistress performeth her ablutions in the sight of the Lord. At this moment may I not open.
VOICE OF CAPTAIN: An thou open not, it shall cost thee.
VOICE OF SERVANT: Nay, now, is not my mistress King's daughter, and is not her command laid on me? O Captain, wilt thou hold it against me, who tremble between two terrors?
VOICE OF CAPTAIN: Tremble shalt thou, when the terror nips thee. E'en open the door, lest we break it in.
VOICE OF SERVANT: Oh, what uncouth man is this, that will break down the door of the King's daughter, and she naked at her bath, before the Lord!
VOICE OF CAPTAIN: We do but the King's bidding.
VOICE OF SERVANT: How can that be? What, did the King indeed bid ye break down the door of his daughter's house, and she uncovered in the Lord's sight, at her ablutions?

VOICE OF CAPTAIN: Yea! The King bade us bring before him instantly the bed of David, and David upon the bed!

VOICE OF SERVANT: Oh, now, what unseemly thing is this! Hath not the King legs long enough? And can he not walk hither on his feet? Oh, send, fetch the King, I pray thee, thou Captain. Say, I pray thee, that Michal prays the King come hither.

VOICE OF CAPTAIN: Word shall be sent. Yet open now this door, that the bird escapes me not.

VOICE OF SERVANT: O Captain! And is my master then a bird? O would he were, even the young eagle, that he might spread wing! O man, hast thou no fear what may befall thee, that thou namest David a bird? O Israel, uncover now thine ear!

VOICE OF CAPTAIN: I name him not.

VOICE OF SERVANT: And what would ye, with this bird my master! Oh, the Lord forbid that any man should call him a bird!

VOICE OF CAPTAIN: We e'en must bring him upon his bed before the King.

VOICE OF SERVANT: Now what is this! Will the King heal him with mighty spells? Or is David on his sick-bed to be carried before the people, that they may know his plight? What new wonder is this?

VOICE OF CAPTAIN: I cannot say—— Yet I will wait no longer.

MICHAL: Open, Maiden! Let them come up.

VOICE OF SERVANT: Oh, my mistress crieth unto me, that I open. Yea, O Michal, I will e'en open to these men. For who dare look aslant at the King's daughter?

CAPTAIN [*entering, followed by* SOLDIERS]: Is David still in the bed? An he cannot rise, will we carry him upon the bed, before the King.

MICHAL: Now what is this?

CAPTAIN: Sleeps he yet? Ho, David, sleepest thou?

2ND SOLDIER: We will take up the bed, and wake him.

3RD SOLDIER: He stirs not at all.

CAPTAIN [*to* MICHAL]: Yea, rouse him and tell him the King's will.

MICHAL: I will not rouse him.

CAPTAIN [*going to the bed*]: Ho, thou! Ho! David! [*He suddenly pulls back the bed-cover.*] What is this? [*Sudden loud shrilling laughter from the* WOMAN-SERVANT, *who flees when the men look round.*]

SOLDIERS [*crowding*]: We are deceived. Ha-ha! It is a man of wood and a goat's-hair bolster! Ha-ha-ha! What husband is this of Michal's?

MICHAL: My teraphim, and the god of my house.

CAPTAIN: Where hast thou hidden David?

MICHAL: I have not hidden him.

Pause

VOICE OF SAUL [*on the stair*]: Why tarry ye here? What! Must the King come on his own errands? [SAUL *enters.*] And are ye here?

MICHAL: The Lord strengthen thee, my Father.

SAUL: Ha! Michal! And can then David not rise from his bed, when the King sendeth for him?

CAPTAIN: Lo! O King! Behold the sick man on the bed! We are deceived of Michal.

SAUL: What is this? [*Flings the image across the room.*]

Scene XIV · DAVID

MICHAL: Oh, my teraphim! Oh, god of my house! Oh, alas, alas, now will misfortune fall on my house! Oh, woe is! woe is me! [*Kneels before teraphim.*]

SAUL: Where is David? Why hast thou deceived me?

MICHAL: O god of my house, god of my mother's house, visit it not upon me!

SAUL: Answer me, or I will slay thee!

MICHAL: God of my house, I am slain! I am slain!

SAUL: Where is David?

MICHAL: O my lord, he is gone; he is gone ere the sun made day.

SAUL: Yea, thou hast helped him against me.

MICHAL [*weeping*]: Oh! Oh! He said unto me: *Let me go; why shouldst thou make me slay thee, to trouble my face in the sight of men.* I could not hinder him, he would have slain me there!

SAUL: Why hast thou deceived me so, and sent away mine enemy, that he is escaped?

MICHAL [*weeping*]: I could not prevent him.

SAUL: Even when did he go?

MICHAL: He rose up before the Lord, in the deep night. And then he would away, while no man saw.

SAUL: Whither is he gone?

MICHAL: Verily, and verily, I know not.

Pause

SAUL: So! He hath escaped me! And my flesh and my blood hath helped mine enemy. Woe to you, Michal! Woe to you! Who have helped your father's enemy, who would pull down thy father to the ground. Lo! my flesh and my blood rebel against me, and my seed lies in wait for me, to make me fall!

MICHAL: Oh, why must David be slain?

SAUL: Woe to you, Michal! And David shall bring woe to you, and woe upon you. David shall pull down Saul, and David shall pull down Jonathan; thee, Michal, he will pull down, yea, and all thy house. Oh, thou mayst call on the teraphim of thy house. But if thy teraphim love thy house, then would he smite David speedily to the death, for if David liveth I shall not live, and thou shalt not live, and thy brother shall not live. For David will bring us all down in blood.

MICHAL [*weeping*]: O my Father, prophesy not against him!

SAUL: It shall be so. What, have I no insight into the dark! And thou art now a woman abandoned of her man, and thy father casteth thee off, because thou hast deceived him, and brought about his hurt.

MICHAL: O my Father, forgive me! Hold it not against me!

SAUL: Nay, thou hast bent thy will against thy father, and called destruction upon thy father's house.

MICHAL: Ah, no! Ah, no!

CURTAIN

SCENE XV

Naioth in Ramah. A round, pyramid-like hill, with a stairlike way to the top, where is a rude rock altar. Many PROPHETS, *young and old, wild and dressed in blue ephods without mantle, on the summit of the hill and down the slope. Some have harps, psalteries, pipes and tabrets. There is wild music and rough, ragged chanting. They are expecting something. Below,* SAMUEL *and* DAVID, *talking. Not far off a* PROPHET *in attendance.*

PROPHETS [*on hill—irregularly crying and chanting*]: This is the place of the Lord! Upon us shines the Unseen! Yea, here is very God! Who dare come into the glory! O thou, filled with the Lord, sing with me on this high place. For the egg of the world is filled with God.

SAMUEL [*speaking to* DAVID]: It is time thou shouldst go. As a fox with the dogs upon him, hast thou much fleeing to do.

DAVID: Must I always flee, my Father? I am already weary of flight.

SAMUEL: Yea, to flee away is thy portion. Saul cometh hither to seek thee. But surely shall he fall before the Lord. When he gets him back to his own city, enquire thou what is his will towards thee. And if it still be evil, then flee from him diligently, while he lives.

DAVID: And shall there never be peace between Saul's house and mine?

SAMUEL: Who knows the Lord utterly! If there be not peace this time, then shall there never in life be peace between thee and him, nor thy house and his.

DAVID: Yet am I his son-in-law, in Michal my wife! And my flesh yearneth unto mine own.

SAMUEL: Is the house of Saul thine own?

DAVID: Yea, verily!

SAMUEL: Dost thou say, *Yea, verily?* Hark, now! If this time there be peace between thee and him, it should be peace. But if not, then think of naught but to flee, and save thyself, and keep on fleeing while Saul yet liveth. The Lord's choice is on thee, and thou shalt be King in thy day. As for me, I shall never see thy day.

DAVID: Would I could make my peace with Saul! Would I could return to mine own house, and to mine own wife, and to the men of my charge!

SAMUEL: My son, once the Lord chose Saul. Now hath He passed Saul over and chosen thee. Canst thou look guiltless into the face of Saul? Can he look guiltless into thy face? Can ye look into each other's face, as men who are open and at peace with one another?

DAVID: Yet would I serve him faithfully.

SAMUEL: Yea, verily! And in thine heart, art thou King, and pullest the crown from his brow with thine eyes.

DAVID: O my Father, I would not!

SAMUEL: Wouldst thou not? Willst thou say to me here

Scene XV   DAVID   117

and now: *As the Lord liveth, I will not be King! But Saul and his house shall rule Israel for ever: and Jonathan my friend shall be King over me!* Wilt thou say that to me?

DAVID: Does Samuel bid me say this thing?

SAMUEL: He bids thee not. But for Saul's sake, and for Jonathan's, and for Michal's, and for peace, wilt thou say it? Answer me from thine own heart, for I know the smell of false words. Yea, I bid thee, speak!

DAVID: The Lord shall do unto me as He will.

SAMUEL: Yea, for the Lord hath anointed thee, and thou shalt rule Israel when Saul is dead, and I am dead, and the Judges of Israel are passed away. For my day is nearly over, and thine is another day. Yea, Saul has lived in my day, but thou livest in thine own day, that I know not of.

DAVID: O my lord, is there naught but wrath and sorrow between me and Saul henceforth?

SAMUEL: The Lord will show! Knowest thou not?

DAVID: I would it were peace!

SAMUEL: Wouldst thou verily? When the wind changes, will it not push the clouds its own way? Will fire leap lively in wet rain? The Lord is all things. And Saul hath seen a tall and rushing flame and hath gone mad, for the flame rushed over him. Thou seest thy God in thine own likeness, afar off, or as a brother beyond thee, who fulfils thy desire. Saul yearneth for the flame: thou for thy to-morrow's glory. The God of Saul hath no face. But thou wilt bargain with thy God. So be it! I am old, and would have done. Flee thou, flee, and flee again, and once more flee. So shalt thou at last have the kingdom and the glory in the sight of men. I anointed thee, but I would see thee no more, for my heart is weary of its end.

DAVID: Wilt thou not bless me?

SAMUEL: Yea, I will bless thee! Yea, I will bless thee, my son. Yea, for now thy way is the way of might, yea, and even for a long space of time it shall be so. But after many days, men shall come again to the faceless flame of my Strength, and of Saul's. Yea, I will bless thee! Thou art brave, and alone, and by cunning must thou live, and by cunning shall thy house live for ever. But hath not the Lord created the fox, and the weasel that boundeth and skippeth like a snake!

DAVID: O Samuel, I have but tried to be wise! What should I do, and how should I walk in the sight of men? Tell me, my Father, and I will do it.

SAMUEL: Thou wilt not. Thou walkest wisely, and thy Lord is with thee. Yea, each man's Lord is his own, though God be but one. I know not thy Lord. Yet walk thou with Him. Yea, thou shalt bring a new day for Israel. Yea, thou shalt be great, thou shalt fight as a flower fighteth upwards, through the stones and alone with God, to flower in the sun at last. For the yearning of the Lord streameth as a sun, even upon the stones. [*A tumult above among the* PROPHETS. SAMUEL *looks up—continues abstractedly.*] Yea, and as a flower thou shalt fade. But Saul was once a burning bush, afire with God. Alas, that he saw his own image mirrored in the faces of men! [*A blare of music above.*]

SAMUEL [*to* PROPHET]: What see ye?

PROPHETS [*shouting*]: The sun on the arms of the King.

Scene XV DAVID

SAMUEL [*to* DAVID]: Now shalt thou go! For I, too, will not set mine eyes upon Saul the King.

DAVID: Bless me then, O my Father!

SAMUEL: The Lord fill thy heart and thy soul! The Lord quicken thee! The Lord kindle thy spirit, so thou fall into no snare! And now get thee gone! And when Saul is returned to his own place, enquire thou secretly his will towards thee. And then act wisely, as thou knoweth.

DAVID: I go forth into the fields, as a hare when the hound gives mouth! But if the Lord go with me . . .
 [*Exit.*]

SAMUEL [*to* PROPHET]: Is Saul surely in sight?

PROPHET: Verily, he is not far off. He has passed the well of Shecu.

SAMUEL: Has he company of men?

PROPHET: Ten armed men has he.

SAMUEL: Will he still bring armed men to the high place? Lo! Say thou to him: Samuel hath gone before the Lord, in the hidden places of the Hill.

PROPHET: I will e'en say it.

SAMUEL: Say also to him: David, the anointed, is gone, we know not whither. And let the company of the prophets come down towards the King.

PROPHET: It shall be so.
 [*Exit* SAMUEL.]

PROPHET [*climbing hill and calling*]: O ye Prophets of the Lord, put yourselves in array, to meet Saul the King.

2ND PROPHET [*on hill with flute—sounds flute loudly with a strong tune—shouts*]: Oh, come, all ye that know our God! Oh, put yourselves in array, ye that know the Name. For that which is without name is lovelier than anything named! [*Sounds the tune strongly.*]

[PROPHETS *gather in array—musicians in front; they chant slowly. As* SAUL *approaches they slowly descend.*]

CHORUS OF PROPHETS: Armies there are, for the Lord our God!
Armies there are against the Lord!
Wilt thou shake spears in the face of Almighty God?
Lo! in thy face shakes the lightning.   *Bis*
Countest thou thyself a strong man, sayest thou Ha-ha!
Lo! We are strong in the Lord! Our arrow seest thou not!
Yet with the unseen arrows of high heaven
Pierce we the wicked man's feet, pierce we his feet in the fight.
Lo! the bow of our body is strung by God.
Lo! how He taketh aim with arrow-heads of our wrath!
Prophet of God is an arrow in full flight
And he shall pierce thy shield, thou, thou Lord's enemy.
Long is the fight, yet the unseen arrows fly
Keen to a wound in the soul of the great Lord's enemy.
Slowly he bleeds, yet the red drops run away
Unseen and inwardly, as bleeds the wicked man.
Bleeding of God! Secretly of God.
SAUL [*entering with* ARMED MEN—PROPHETS *continue to chant*]: Peace be with you!
PROPHET: Peace be with the King!

SAUL: Lo! ye prophets of God! Is not Samuel set over you?

PROPHET: Yea! O King!

SAUL [*beginning to come under the influence of the chant and to take the rhythm in his voice*]: Is Samuel not here?

PROPHET: He hath gone up before the Lord!

SAUL: Surely the Lord is in this place! Surely the great brightness [*looks round*]—and the son of Jesse, is he among the prophets?

PROPHET: Nay, he has gone hence.

SAUL: Gone! Gone! What, has he fled from the high place! Surely he feared the glory! Yea, the brightness! So he has fled before the flame! Thus shall he flee before the flame! But gone? Whither gone?

PROPHET: We know not whither.

SAUL: Even let him go! Even let him go whither he will! Yea, even let him go! Yea! Come we forth after such as he? Let him go! Is not the Lord here? Surely the brightness is upon the hill! Surely it gleams upon this high place!

LEADER OF MEN-AT-ARMS: Tarry we here, O King? Where shall we seek the son of Jesse?

SAUL: Even where ye will.

LEADER: Tarrieth the King here?

SAUL: Yea! I will know if the Lord is verily in this place.

PROPHET: Verily He is here.

[*Company of* PROPHETS *still chant.*]

SAUL [*going slowly forward*]: Art Thou here, O Lord? What? Is this Thy brightness upon the hill? What? Art Thou here in Thy glory?

COMPANY OF PROPHETS: Fire within fire is the presence of the Lord!
    Sun within the sun is our God!   *Bis.*
    Rises the sun among the hills of thy heart
    Rising to shine in thy breast?   *Bis.*
SAUL: Yea! O Prophets! Am I not King? Shall not the Sun of suns rise among the hills of my heart, and make dawn in my body? What! Shall these prophets know the glory of the Lord, and shall the son of Kish stay under a cloud? [*Sticks his spear into the ground, and unbuckles his sword-belt.*]
LEADER OF ARMED MEN: Wilt thou go up before the Lord, O King? Then camp we here, to await thy pleasure.
SAUL: I will go up. Camp an ye will.
LEADER: Even camp we here.
    [*They untackle.*]
SAUL: Ha! Ha! Is there a glory upon the prophets? Do their voices resound like rocks in the valley! Ha! Ha! Thou of the sudden fire! I am coming! Yea! I will come into the glory! [*Advancing, throws down his woollen mantle. The* 1ST PROPHET *takes it up.*]
CHORUS OF PROPHETS: Whiteness of wool helps thee not in the high place,
    Colours on thy coat avail thee naught.   *Bis.*
    Fire unto fire only speaks, and only flame
    Beckons to flame of the Lord!   *Bis.*
    [*The* PROPHETS *divide and make way as* SAUL *comes up.*]
SAUL: Is my heart a cold hearth? Is my heart fireless unto Thee? Kindler! it shall not be so! My heart shall shine to Thee, yea, unshadow itself. Yea, the

fire in me shall mount to the fire of Thee, Thou Wave of Brightness!

SOLDIER [*below—with loud and sudden shout*]: The sun is in my heart. Lo! I shine forth!

SAUL [*with suddenness*]: I will come up! Oh! I will come up! Dip me in the flame of brightness, Thou Bright One, call up the sun in my heart, out of the clouds of me. Lo! I have been darkened and deadened with ashes! Blow a fierce flame on me, from the middle of Thy glory, O Thou of the faceless flame. [*Goes slowly forward.*] Oh, dip me in the ceaseless flame!

[*Throws down his coat, or wide-sleeved tunic, that came below the knee and was heavily embroidered at neck and sleeves in many colours: is seen in the sleeveless shirt that comes half way down the thigh.*]

SOLDIER [*below*]: Kings come and pass away, but the flame is flame forever. The Lord is here, like a tree of white fire! Yea, and the white glory goes in my nostrils like a scent.

SAUL: Shall a soldier be more blessed than I? Lo! I am not dead, thou Almighty! My flesh is still flame, still steady flame. Flame to flame calleth, and that which is dead is cast away. [*Flings off his shirt: is seen, a dark-skinned man in leathern loin-girdle.*] Nay, I carry naught upon me, the long flame of my body leans to the flame of all glory! I am no king, save in the Glory of God. I have no kingdom, save my body and soul. I have no name. But as a slow and dark flame leaneth to a great glory of flame, and is sipped up, naked and nameless lean I to the glory of the Lord.

CHORUS OF PROPHETS: Standeth a man upon the stem
of upright knees
> Openeth the navel's closed bud, unfoldeth the
> flower of the breast!
> Lo! Like the cup of a flower, with morning sun
> Filled is thy breast with the Lord, filled is thy
> navel's wide flower!

SOLDIER: Oh, come! For a little while the glory of the Lord stands upon the high place! Oh, come! before they build Him houses, and enclose Him within a roof! Oh, it is good to live now, with the light of the first day's sun upon the breast. For when the seed of David have put the Lord inside a house, the glory will be gone, and men will walk with no transfiguration! Oh, come to this high place! Oh, come!

SAUL: Surely I feel my death upon me! Surely the sleep of sleeps descends. [*Casts himself down.*] I cast myself down, night and day; as in death, lie I naked before God. Ah, what is life to me! Alas that a man must live till death visit him!—that he cannot walk away into the cloud of Sun! Alas for my life! For my children and my children's children, alas! For the son of Jesse will wipe them out! Alas for Israel! For the fox will trap the lion of strength, and the weasel that is a virgin, and bringeth forth her young from her mouth, shall be at the throats of brave men! Yea, by cunning shall Israel prosper, in the days of the seed of David: and by cunning and lurking in holes of the earth shall the seed of Jesse fill the earth. Then the Lord of Glory will have drawn far off, and gods shall be pitiful, and men shall be as locusts. But I, I feel my death upon me,

Scene XV   DAVID   125

even in the glory of the Lord. Yea, leave me in peace
before my death, let me retreat into the flame!

A pause

ANOTHER SOLDIER: Saul hath abandoned his kingdom
and his men! Yea, he puts the Lord between him
and his work!
PROPHET: E'en let him be! For his loss is greater than
another's triumph.
SOLDIER: Yea! But wherefore shall a man leave his
men leaderless—even for the Lord!
1ST SOLDIER [*prophesying*]: When thou withdrawest
Thy glory, let me go with Thee, O Brightest, even
into the fire of Thee!
CHORUS OF PROPHETS: Cast thyself down, that the Lord
  may snatch thee up.
Fall before the Lord, and fall high.
All things come forth from the flame of Almighty
  God,
Some things shall never return! [*Bis.*]
Some have their way and their will, and pass at last
To the worm's waiting mouth. [*Bis.*]
But the high Lord He leans down upon the hill,
And wraps His own in His flame,
Wraps them as whirlwind from the world,
Leaves not one sigh for the grave. . . .

CURTAIN

SCENE XVI

Late afternoon. A rocky place outside Gilgal. DAVID *is hiding near the stone Ezel.*

DAVID [*alone*]: Now, if Jonathan comes not, I am lost. This is the fourth day, and evening is nigh. Lo! Saul seeketh my life. O Lord, look upon me, and hinder mine enemies! Frustrate them, make them stumble, O my God! So near am I to Gilgal, yet between me and mine own house lies the whole gap of death. Yea, Michal, thou art not far from me. Yet art thou distant even as death. I hide and have hidden. Three days have I hidden, and eaten scant bread. Lo! Is this to be the Lord's anointed! Saul will kill me, and I shall die! There! Someone moves across the field! Ah, watch! watch! Is it Jonathan? It is two men; yea, it is two men. And one walks before the other. Surely it is Jonathan and his lad! Surely he has kept his word! O Lord, save me now from mine enemies, for they compass me round. O Lord my God, put a rope round the neck of my enemy, lest he rush forward and seize me in the secret place. Yea, it is Jonathan, in a striped coat. And a man behind him carryeth the bow. Yea, now must I listen, and uncover my ears, for this is life or death. O that he may say: *Behold, the arrows are on this side of thee, take them!* For then I can come forth and go to my house, and the King will look kindly on me.—But he comes slowly, and sadly. And he will say: *The arrows are beyond thee*—and I shall have to flee away like a hunted dog, into the desert.—It will be so! Yea! And I must hide lest that lad who follows Jonathan should see me, and set Saul's soldiery upon me. [*Exit after a pause.*]

[*Enter* JONATHAN *with bow, and* LAD *with quiver.*]

JONATHAN [*stringing his bow*]: Lo! this is the stone Ezel. Seest thou the dead bush, like a camel's head? That is a mark I have shot at, and now, before the light falls, will I put an arrow through his nose. [*Takes an arrow.*] Will this fly well? [*Balancing it.*]

LAD: It is well shafted, O Jonathan.

JONATHAN: Ay! Let us shoot. [*Takes aim—shoots.*] Yea, it touched the camel's ear, but not his nose! Give me another! [*Shoots.*] Ah! Hadst thou a throat, thou camel, thou wert dead. Yet is thy nose too cheerful! Let us try again! [*Takes another arrow—shoots.*] Surely there is a scratch upon thy nose-tip! Nay, I am not myself! Give me the quiver. And run thou, take up the arrows ere the shadows come.

LAD: I will find them.

[*He runs, as he goes* JONATHAN *shoots an arrow over his head. The* LAD *runs after it—stops.*]

JONATHAN: Is not the arrow beyond thee?

LAD: One is here! Here, another!

JONATHAN: The arrow is beyond thee! Make speed! Haste! Stay not!

LAD: Three have I! But the fourth——

JONATHAN: The arrow is beyond thee! Run, make haste!

LAD: I see it not! I see it not! Yea, it is there within bush. I have it, and it is whole. O master, is this all?

JONATHAN: There is one more. Behold it is beyond thee.

LAD [*running*]: I see it not! I see it not! Yea, it is here!

JONATHAN: It is all. Come, then! Come! Nay, the light is fading and I cannot see. Take thou the bow and the arrows, and go home. For I will rest here awhile by the stone Ezel.

LAD: Will my master come home alone?

JONATHAN: Yea will I, with the peace of day's-end upon me. Go now, and wait me in the house. I shall soon come.

[*Exit* LAD. JONATHAN *sits down on a stone till he is gone.*]

JONATHAN [*calling softly*]: David! David!

[DAVID *comes forth, weeping. Falls on his face to the ground and bows himself three times before* JONATHAN. JONATHAN *raises him. They kiss one another, and weep.*]

DAVID: Ah, then it is death, it is death to me from Saul?

JONATHAN: Yea, he seeks thy life, and thou must flee far hence.

DAVID [*weeping*]: Ah, Jonathan! Thy servant thanks thee from his heart. But ah, Jonathan, it is bitter to go, to flee like a dog, to be houseless and homeless and wifeless, without a friend or helpmate! Oh, what have I done, what have I done! Tell me, what have I done! And slay me if I be in fault.

JONATHAN [*in tears*]: Thou art not in fault. Nay, thou art not! But thou art anointed, and thou shalt be King. Hath not Samuel said it even now, in Naioth, when he would not look upon the face of Saul! Yea, thou must flee until thy day come, and the day of the death of Saul, and the day of the death of Jonathan.

DAVID [*weeping*]: Oh, I have not chosen this. This have I not taken upon myself. This is put upon me, I have not chosen it! I do not want to go! Yea, let me come to Gilgal and die, so I see thy face, and the face of Michal, and the face of the King. Let me die! Let me come to Gilgal and die! [*Flings himself on the ground in a paroxysm of grief.*]

JONATHAN: Nay! Thou shalt not die. Thou shalt flee! And till Saul be dead, thou shalt flee. But when Saul has fallen, and I have fallen with my father—for even now my life follows my father—then thou shalt be King.

DAVID: I cannot go!

JONATHAN: Yea! Thou shalt go now. For they will send forth men to meet me, ere the dark. Rise now, and be comforted. [DAVID *rises.*]

DAVID: Why shouldst thou save me! Why dost thou withhold thy hand! Slay me now!

JONATHAN: I would not slay thee, nor now nor ever. But leave me now, and go. And go in peace, forasmuch as we have sworn both of us in the name of the Lord, saying: *The Lord be between me and thee, and between my seed and thy seed for ever.*

DAVID: Yea, the covenant is between us! And I will go, and keep it.

[*They embrace in silence, and in silence* DAVID *goes out.*]

JONATHAN [*alone in the twilight*]: Thou goest, David! And the hope of Israel with thee! I remain, with my father, and the star-stone falling to despair. Yet what is it to me! I would not see thy new day, David. For thy wisdom is the wisdom of the subtle, and behind thy passion lies prudence. And naked thou wilt not go into the fire. Yea, go thou forth, and let me die. For thy virtue is in thy wit, and thy shrewdness. But in Saul have I known the magnanimity of a man. Yea, thou art a smiter down of giants, with a smart stone! Great men and magnanimous, men of the faceless flame, shall fall from Strength, fall before thee, thou David, shrewd whelp of the lion of Judah! Yet my heart yearns hot over thee, as over a tender, quick child. And the heart of my father yearns, even amid its dark wrath. But thou goest forth, and knowest no depth of yearning, thou son of Jesse. Yet go! For my twilight is more to me than thy day, and my death is dearer to me than thy life! Take it! Take thou the kingdom, and the days to come. In the flames of death where Strength is, I will wait and watch till the day of David at last shall be finished, and wisdom no more be fox-faced, and the blood gets back its flame. Yea, the flame dies not, though the sun's red dies! And I must get me to the city.

[*Rises and departs hastily.*]

CURTAIN

www.ingramcontent.com/pod-product-compliance
Lightning Source LLC
Chambersburg PA
CBHW011951150426
43195CB00018B/2889